Stand Up If You Hate Man United

Kick-off

We would like to thank our wives Liz Setterfield and
Luise Finan, editor Sarah Such, her assistants
Anna-Maria Watters and Mary Wessel,
designer Stuart Brill, David Taylor and Toby Stevens
for helping with our research. Most of all, we would
like to thank Manchester United Football Club, its
players, managers, officials, and supporters,
past and present.

4

Stand Up If You Hate
Man United

SIMON BULLIVANT AND BILL MATTHEWS

NEW ENGLISH LIBRARY

First published in Great Britain in 1998
by New English Library
A division of Hodder Headline PLC

10 9 8 7 6 5 4 3 2 1

A CIP Catalogue record is available from the British Library.

ISBN 0 340 71754 8

The publishers would like to thank the following for permission to
reproduce copyright material. While every effort has been made to
trace and acknowledge all copyright holders, we would like to
apologise should there have been any errors or omissions.

Photographs:

Coloursport, Hulton Getty, Mirror Syndication, News International,
PA News, Popperfoto, ProSport International, Solo Syndication

Designed by the Senate
Illustrations by David Parkins

Printed and bound in Great Britain by
Butler & Tanner Ltd, Frome and London

New English Library
A division of Hodder Headline PLC
338 Euston Road
London NW1 3BH

Contents

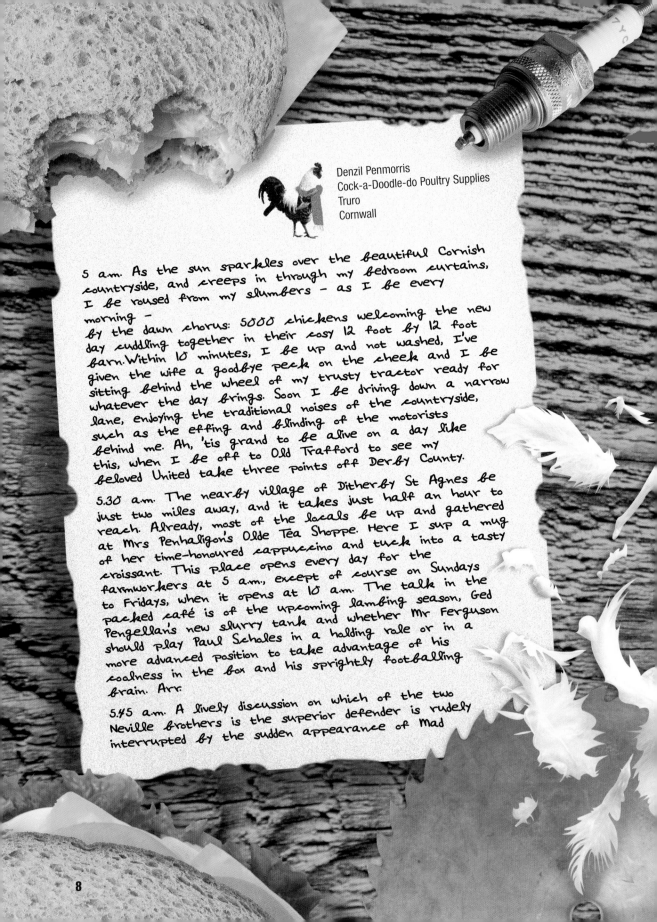

Denzil Penmorris
Cock-a-Doodle-do Poultry Supplies
Truro
Cornwall

5 a.m. As the sun sparkles over the beautiful Cornish countryside, and creeps in through my bedroom curtains, I be roused from my slumbers – as I be every morning –

by the dawn chorus: 5000 chickens welcoming the new day cuddling together in their cosy 12 foot by 12 foot barn. Within 10 minutes, I be up and not washed, I've given the wife a goodbye peck on the cheek and I be sitting behind the wheel of my trusty tractor ready for whatever the day brings. Soon I be driving down a narrow lane, enjoying the traditional noises of the countryside, such as the effing and blinding of the motorists behind me. Ah, 'tis grand to be alive on a day like this, when I be off to Old Trafford to see my beloved United take three points off Derby County.

5.30 a.m. The nearby village of Ditherby St Agnes be just two miles away, and it takes just half an hour to reach. Already, most of the locals be up and gathered at Mrs Penhaligon's Olde Tea Shoppe. Here I sup a mug of her time-honoured cappuccino and tuck into a tasty croissant. This place opens every day for the farmworkers at 5 a.m., except of course on Sundays to Fridays, when it opens at 10 a.m. The talk in the packed café is of the upcoming lambing season, Ged Pengellan's new slurry tank and whether Mr Ferguson should play Paul Scholes in a holding role or in a more advanced position to take advantage of his coolness in the box and his sprightly footballing brain. Arr.

5.45 a.m. A lively discussion on which of the two Neville brothers is the superior defender is rudely interrupted by the sudden appearance of Mad

Tom, the Village Idiot. The place goes
so quiet, you'd think a tourist had wandered
in and asked for directions. We feel more
pity than hatred for Mad Tom and have
tried many times to make him see where he's
gone wrong in his life. But no – he still
insists on supporting the local team.

6 a.m. The honk of a hooter outside tells us it be
time to go on the coach. Sadly, it be a poor show
from the village this week, as only ten coaches
are needed for the trip up to Manchester.
Unfortunately, Ted Pendleton and his lads are staying
behind to shoot several hundred BSE-infected cattle
and sell the meat abroad before the inspectors
arrive tomorrow. And they call themselves football
fans.

6.15 a.m. We be off at last. As we leave the
village square, I catches a glimpse of poor old
Willie Penmarrow shuffling past the Ferguson &
Firkin. What a sad sight he be – homeless,
destitute and wearing last season's away kit. If only
he'd filled in that EC form 3ZC/E4, he'd still be
coining half a million a year in subsidies. Well, no
one said farming was easy.

1 p.m. Some people might think it be an odd way to
spend every Saturday, stuck in a coach for seven
hours at a stretch – but my time is not wasted.
Using my faithful Dell portable Pentium computer,
equipped with fax/modem, I be never out of touch
with the farm. With a click on the mouse, I
can adjust the farm's fully automated feed
system, while joining in a rousing chorus of
'There Be Only One Jaap Stam.'
  Not only that, I can also email
  the missus and tell her I
  hopes to be home by
  midnight.

MANAGER
WILF McGUINNESS

1969–70

When Sir Matt Busby retired after 24 years as manager in April 1969, he chose his own successor carefully. A 31-year-old former Busby Babe whose career had been cut short by injury, but whom Sir Matt had kept on as assistant trainer. He owed everything to his mentor. What a lucky man Wilf McGuinness was, everyone thought, to be stepping into Sir Matt Busby's shoes. The only problem was, Sir Matt hadn't yet stepped out of them.

The European Cup winning team of 1968 seemed to believe they had a job for life. For a number of reasons, it was difficult for McGuinness to earn the respect of his players. He had an ageing team who had long traded on past glories – ones that he had missed out on. A number of them, such as Bobby Charlton and Paddy Crerand, were his contemporaries. Any attempt by McGuinness to drop a senior player would invariably result in his bleating to Sir Matt, who would advise McGuinness to reverse the decision. He didn't help himself by continuing to refer to Busby as 'Boss'. What were the players supposed to call him?

The beginning of the end came just a handful of matches into his reign, when he dared to drop Bobby Charlton and Denis Law for a match against Everton. After a 3–0 defeat, a journalist who asked McGuinness to explain the reason was told by him to go and talk to Sir Matt. These players would always be associated with the previous manager, so that if they were successful the credit would go to Busby, but if they flopped, it would inevitably be put down to McGuinness' failure to get the best out of them.

United suffered a poor start to the 1970–71 season, and by December they were languishing in 18th place. The death knell came with a 2–1 defeat in a League Cup semi-final against Aston Villa, which might sound respectable enough, except that in those days Villa were a Third Division team. The United board were sensitive enough not to sack McGuinness just before Christmas; they got shot of

him just after Christmas instead. Merry Christmas, Wilf. Thanks, Boss.

McGuinness returned from whence he came, and became trainer-coach of the reserves, while Sir Matt slipped back into those shoes he'd never really taken off in the first place. Within two months, McGuinness had left the club altogether. After three years coaching in Greece, he returned to England in 1974. The following year he put all his bad luck at United behind him when he accepted his most prestigious job in English football, becoming manager of York City.

WHAT WENT WRONG AT BIG-TIME UNITED?

I believe McGuinness's problems started when he decided to drop Bobby Charlton for an away match at Everton last season.

They were close friends since boyhood and rightly or wrongly some of the players believe that McGuinness sacrificed that friendship to hammer home to all the players that he was boss.

For weeks the football grapevine in Manchester has buzzed with a persistent story that the players had signed a round robin asking the club to relieve McGuinness of his job.

When this was put to Busby yesterday he said 'I cannot and will not answer that sort of question.'

To be fair to Wilf McGuinness, however, it must be made clear that when he took over, he inherited a side that had reached its peak and was on the way down.

The *Sun*, 30 December 1970

Manchester United broke Wilf McGuinness' heart and made him lose his hair.

Now he says, 'They didn't give me the time to do the job. They'd promised me three years. When I go back there, I can be friendly with Matt. But there's something in my head that says 'You didn't give me the support when I needed it.'

The *Sun*, 19 December 1989

£1 BRYAN ROBSON £1
INACTION FIGURE™

FOR THE FIRST TIME, your chance to own a lasting souvenir of Bryan Robson's memorable years at Manchester United! Fully broken from head to toe, your Bryan Robson Inaction Figure™ is guaranteed to fall apart as soon as it's been put together. When you pull any part of his body, the Inaction Figure speaks a number of phrases, 'I'll be fit for Saturday, boss', 'Ouch!', 'Oh no, it's gone again' and 'Send for my faith healer'.

Discover why Bryan Robson was nicknamed 'Pop', after hearing the authentic sound of another bone coming out of its socket. Marvel at the stunning detail! There's no stone left unturned or bone left uncrushed. All genuine injuries, as authenticated by the Manchester United physio.

Head – Concussed in January 1988 when he collided with QPR's Danny Maddix.

Shoulder – Dislocated v Coventry in 1985, v West Ham in 1986, then again v Morocco when his tireless running took him into the advertising hoardings, World Cup 1986. Missed rest of tournament.

Back – Damaged sciatic nerve, diagnosed 1992.

Hamstring – Torn v Turkey in 1985, then recurred a month later v Sheffield Wednesday. Then again v Coventry in 1986. Yet again v Norwich also in 1986. Yet yet again v Celtic in 1992.

Leg muscles – Strained v Chelsea, 1988.

Ligaments – Torn medial ligaments v Arsenal, 1983.

Fibula – Fractured v Portsmouth, 1989.

Ankle – Damaged v West Ham, 1986.

Instep – Badly bruised v Oxford in 1983.

Ear – Infected after sinus operation, 1993. Played on. 'It's only an ear,' he said.

Nose – Broken on South American tour in 1984, then again in 1987 v West Ham.

Mouth – Gashed v QPR, 1989.

Ribs – Bruised v Derby County, 1989.

Hernia – Went in practice match, 1990.

Groin – Pulled v Liverpool, 1989.

Thigh – Damaged v Charlton 1987. Then again in shooting practice with Peter Shilton, 1988.

Calf – Went in pre-season training in Norway, 1990.

Achilles tendon – Inflamed v Holland in 1990 World Cup. Missed rest of tournament.

Left foot – Blistered v QPR, 1987.

Halifax Town	2	1	Manchester United

Atkins, Wallace (pen.)   19,765   Best (pen.)

Watney Mann Invitation Cup 1st round, 31 July 1971

Halifax Town, then of the Third Division, dumped United in the greatest upset in the Watney Cup's two-year history. Admittedly this was a bit of a Mickey Mouse tournament – rather like today's Auto Windscreens Shield or European Cup Winners' Cup. The entry qualifications were quite straightforward: the two highest-scoring teams in each of the four divisions which hadn't been promoted, relegated, won the League or qualified for Europe played each other in a knockout competition. United's ageing side, featuring one of the earliest sightings of Bobby Charlton with long hair, discovered that The Shay in late July is never an easy place to get a result.

Having won the European Cup just three years before, the Watney Cup was clearly the competition United now most wanted to win. The previous season they had reached the Final by seeing off Hull City, a victory that bore all the hallmarks of Man United in the 1990s: a late equaliser and a blatant penalty denied in the last minute. All that was unusual was that they won a penalty shootout – the first ever in British football. This enabled them to get through to the Final and be annihilated 4–1 by Derby County.

Halifax: Smith, Burgin, Lee, Wallace, Pickering, Rhodes, Chadwick, Atkins, Robertson, Lennard, Holmes
Man Utd: Stepney, Fitzpatrick, Dunne, Crerand (Burns), James, Sadler, Morgan, Gowling (Kidd), Charlton, Law, Best

BOLD HALIFAX SHOCK UNITED

Halifax got away to a lightning start when after three minutes the tall Atkins rose to head home a centre from Chadwick. United had their chance to draw level after 25 minutes when a defender was adjudged to have handled, but Morgan's weak penalty was saved by Smith. United had their chances in the second half, but Law missed twice. Tiring Halifax held on bravely until Best, after being brought down by Pickering, took the penalty himself and scored. This, however, was the extent of United's rally.

Halifax, gallant to the end, well deserved to go through to a semi-final against West Bromwich Albion at The Shay on Wednesday.

GEORGE BEST

NOW YOU SEE HIM, NOW YOU DON'T

George Best played a key role in what is now acknowledged as the greatest period in Manchester United's history. Their decline from a European Cup winning side to a bunch of relegated no-hopers in six short glorious years was mirrored by Best's decline from European Footballer of the Year to a sad unshaven drunk.

In the late 1960s, for opposition defenders it was frequently a case of 'now you see him, now you don't' as they were left bemused and dazzled by Best weaving in and out on his way to goal. By the early 1970s, for United managers, it was more a case of 'now you don't see him at all' as he jinxed this way and that on his way to the bar. To the United fans, Best was a magician, full of amazing tricks, but soon his repertoire had dwindled to one routine – the disappearing act.

January 1971 – This was a month of missing training and missing trains. If only someone had given George a Manchester to London railway timetable for Christmas. A week after he managed to miss a train to the Chelsea game, he missed another one on his way to Lancaster Gate to answer a disrepute charge. Thankfully, he reached London in time to spend the weekend with actress Sinead Cusack. The United management had no idea where Best was, but the gaggle of girls outside Ms Cusack's flat should have been a clue. He was suspended for two weeks by the club.

January 1972 – January in the early 1970s inevitably meant public sector strikes, talk of a Beatles reunion and George Best going AWOL. No matter how drunk or dissolute he was, Bestie was clearly faithful to his New Year's Resolution, 'I must miss more training sessions.' The club fined him two weeks' wages and ordered him to move out of his luxury Cheshire house back into digs with his old landlady Mrs Fullaway. Best was glad to get away. Everything in the dream home he'd had especially built was centrally controlled by a console, including a TV and a stereo system which emerged from the chimney, beer available on pump, and a sunken bath which could fit a small army of blondes. Unfortunately, the bath's generous size meant it could only be filled to a depth of three inches, the house quickly became Cheshire's biggest tourist attraction, and worst of all, whenever an aeroplane flew over the house, all the gadgets were set off.

May 1972 – George broke every rule in the book: he went missing in May instead of January. While his Northern Ireland colleagues were preparing for the Home Internationals, rumour had it that Best was in Malaga. These were vicious and unsubstantiated lies – he was actually in Marbella. His revelations that he was drinking too much, seducing women and staying out till five in the morning must have come as a shock to the public, who had long assumed he was teetotaller, celibate and tucked up in bed by ten. Best also announced his retirement for the first time that year.

September 1972 – George opted to spend a night on the town rather than turn out for Bobby Charlton's testimonial. After all, what had Charlton ever done for Manchester United?

December 1972 – Like Christmas, the buildup to George Best's annual disappearance was starting earlier and earlier. He first missed training in late November and was placed on the transfer list by Frank O'Farrell. He was then taken off the list by the United directors, who sacked O'Farrell a week later.

Coincidentally, on the same day, United also decided to fire George Best. Even more coincidentally, an apparently oblivious Best – his usual state in those days – handed in a letter of resignation.

January 1974 – Three months before, manager Tommy Docherty had persuaded Best to return. At first it seemed like a dream come true – George Best was back in a United shirt and the team were desperately fighting to avoid the drop. On 1 January 1974, George Best played his last ever game for Manchester United at QPR. On 4 January, George failed to show for training – perhaps he'd been out the night before celebrating the third anniversary of his first disappearance. He was put back on the transfer list, which is where – apart from various hotels in Spain – he stayed. The only firm offer to buy him came from Southern League Tonbridge.

'I'll TAKE YUS ALL ON'

BREACH OF PROMISE

In 1970 Sir Matt Busby advised George Best to take a wife (as if he hadn't taken enough already) to 'quieten him down'. A week after meeting Danish model Eva Haraldsted, they were engaged. This was not what Sir Matt had in mind, and George soon broke off the engagement. In one of the last cases of its kind before the law was changed, Eva sued George for breach of promise and won £500.

BARNEY AT BLINKERS

Former fiancée Eva Haraldsted kept turning up at Best's favourite Manchester nightclub, Blinkers. One night she insisted the club DJ play 'Leaving on a jet plane' time and again. George hit back by requesting 'Get back', as in 'Get back to where you once belonged', as a dig at her. One of Eva's friends came into the record booth and grabbed the disc off Best.
A comic scuffle broke out, fists and insults were thrown. 'Leaving on a jet plane' later became George's theme tune.

RUMBLE AT RUBENS

In November 1973, George ended up in court accused of punching a woman in the face after a dispute in Rubens nightclub. His provocation was that Stefanja Sloniecki had, apparently, called him an 'Irish navvy'. His alleged witty response was to suggest that she leave the club and go to a restaurant where prostitutes hang out. He was found guilty of assault but conditionally discharged on payment of £100 damages and costs.

THE BEAUTY AND THE BEST

With ex-Miss World Marjorie Wallace, George Best met his match at last. Instead of competing for a woman's affections with night owls of Manchester, this time he had to fend off the likes of Jimmy Connors and Tom Jones. In April 1974, one of the steadiest relationships of Best's life so far – lasting fully two nights – ended in a courtroom. He was cleared of stealing her Miss World tiara, fur coat and passport, and in the words of the magistrate left the court 'without a stain on his character'. The stain-free Best later admitted to the press that he had pinched her diary. Bestie said, 'She could have become Mrs George Best,' although by this time the chances of a reconciliation were receding. 'Once he opens his mouth, he's just one big yawn,' was Marjorie's loving response.

54 DAYS IN CHOKEY

You can never get a taxi in London when it's raining. This hoary old cliché led to George Best spending Christmas 1984 in Pentonville prison. After a night and most of a morning on the tiles, Best was arrested for drunk-driving. He failed to turn up at the court hearing the next day, which made him a fugitive from the law. After being caught hiding out in a neighbour's house, he was put into a police van, where he allegedly assaulted one of the arresting officers. Best was sent to prison for 12 weeks. He served 54 days, during which he turned down various approaches in the shower – the only time he ever passed up a shag. Deprived of spending the festivities with girlfriend Angie and son Calum, George was comforted by receiving Christmas cards from such luminaries as the Krays, Bernie Winters and Julian Lennon.

Best to have loved and lost...

Angie James
Leggy blonde, mother of Calum, the woman who said, 'I do' and shortly afterwards 'I want a divorce'.

Marjorie Wallace
Leggy, American blonde and Miss World, their court case lasted longer than their relationship.

Carolyn Moore
Leggy, bubble-permed Miss Great Britain, who wisely denied she was engaged to the Belfast boy.

Lynsey de Paul
Leggy, blonde songstress and beauty-spot-wearing Eurovision diva, who hit 'Rock bottom' with Bestie.

Sinead Cusack
Leggy, future Mrs Jeremy Irons – and blonde – with whom George sought comfort and companionship.

Debbie Forsyth
Leggy, blonde daughter of multi-talented Brucie, who briefly allowed George Best the pleasure of her company.

Mary Stavin
Leggy fitness queen, occasional blonde, and another ex-Miss World, her videos with George disappointed some unwary purchasers

Juliet Mills
Daughter of leggy actor Sir John Mills, with whom George had a brief but meaningful dalliance.

BEST ON BEST

'I've been reading Dylan Thomas and poetry. That's what I shall be doing to relax myself. I've been doing some writing too.' **(The Sun, January 1971)**

'I dreaded the cranks who rang me 24 hours a day threatening violence and death, and the giggling girls who rang at 3 a.m.' **(Sunday Times, May 1972)**

'The birds used to shout at me, "Skinny, ugly sod." I used to want to thump them and grab them because it was true. Instead, I put birds out of my mind.' **(Best: An Intimate Biography, 1975)**

'I didn't play golf. It interfered with my sex life.' **(Best: An Intimate Biography, 1975)**

'Tomorrow is my 26th birthday, the day I will always remember as the day I quit soccer.' **(Sunday Mirror, 21 May 1972)**

'I am going to rest, write my autobiography, and go into business as a clothes designer.' **(Sunday Mirror, May 1972)**

'I have decided not to play football again and this time no one will change my mind.' **(Daily Mirror, 19 December 1972)**

'I'm very partial to Scandinavian crumpet, it being generally beautiful, always willing and a bit thick.' **(Best: An Intimate Biography, 1975)**

'For the last year all I've done is drink.' **(Sunday Mirror, December 1972)**

'I ran away to Spain and spent several months lying in the sun and making love to every woman I met.' **(Daily Star, September 1990)**

'It might have been different if I'd married when I was 19 … Marriage would have given me stability, but looking back I can say that at 20 years old it was too late for me.' **(Sunday Mirror, December 1972)**

On the sort of novels he intended to write: 'Well, sort of Dick Francis stuff about football.' **(The Guardian, September 1981)**

(On Eva Haraldsted) 'You could say I fell in love with a pair of knockers.' **(Best: An Intimate Biography, 1975)**

'If you want the secret of my success with women – ignoring the fact that I'm George Best, which always helps – then don't smoke, don't take drugs and don't be too particular.' **(News of the World, February 1975)**

'I hated the press. They used to tell such bloody great lies about me. When I finally gave the game up they all wrote I was drinking a bottle of Scotch a day. Everyone knows I'm a vodka drinker.' **(News of the World, February 1975)**

'I've never taken a drug in my life. Not even an aspirin … Perhaps that was foolish, as I've certainly had some headaches.' **(Daily Express, May 1986)**

OTHERS ON BEST
'Where's George?'
Sir Matt Busby

GEORGE'S MARVELLOUS VENTURES

ENTERPRISES

Edwardia Manchester boutique (with Mike Summerbee). 'For trendy sophisticates'. Opened 1967.

Georgie Girl Boutique in Sale, Cheshire. Opened 1965.

George Best Rogue Manchester city centre boutique. Opened 1969.

Slack Alice Manchester nightclub. Opened 1975.

Bestie's Bar on Hermosa Beach, Los Angeles. Opened 1980.

Blondes Mayfair nightclub. Opened 1986.

ENDORSEMENTS

Egg Marketing Board Slogan 'E for B and Georgie Best'

George Best Soccer Slippers Slippers

Bellair Cosmetics Complaints from customers, 'They didn't want to buy products advertised by him,' said the chairman

Great Universal Stores Modelling contract

Tyne-tex Anoraks

Others Plastic footballs, coffee mugs, chewing gum (his agent said, 'It's not enough for George to lend his name to these things. He's got to like the gum – and he does.')

CHAMPIONSHIP FLOPS

NUMBER ONE

1971-1972

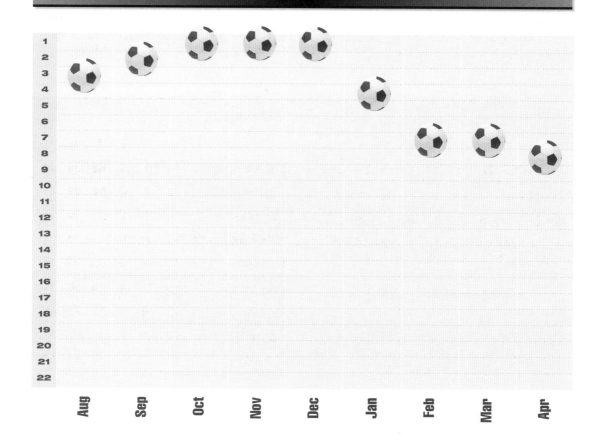

With the millstone of five seasons since they last won the League title hanging round their necks, 1971–2 was surely going to be the campaign when that great burden was finally lifted. The Wilf McGuinness 18 months seemed dim and distant, not to mention hazy and rather a long way away.

Those footballing legends Best, Law and Charlton were all still at the height of their powers, while emerging talents like Ian Donald, Clive Griffiths and Daniel Healey were waiting in the wings to become the new legends at Old Trafford.

On 4 December, their 3–2 win at home to Nottingham Forest took Man United five points clear at the top – and with two points for a win, that was a lot of points in those days. They were seemingly coasting to the title.

Of course that's when it all began to go quite laughably wrong. Three successive draws against humdrum opposition were only a portent. From early January to early March, United lost seven successive League games and plunged from 1st to 9th. In all, they went 11 League matches without a win – a proud post-war club record.

Three wins in a row against the dregs of the division were enough to give them the illusion of being back in the title race. But then three defeats in four over Easter – including a 3–0 home defeat by Liverpool – finally killed off their dreams for another year. After leading the First Division up to the middle of January, it took some doing to finish in 8th.

	P	W	D	L	F	A	Pts
1st half	21	14	5	2	47	25	33
2nd half	21	5	5	11	22	36	15

	Before New Year	After New Year
Best	14	4 (2 pen)
Charlton	5	3
Law	12	1

So the question is, where did Manchester United go wrong? Was it the declining form of George Best, who admitted he'd spent much of the second half of the season very much the worse for wear? Was it Frank O'Farrell's inability to earn the respect of the players? Was it Matt Busby's reluctance to let go? But in the end, the main question is – who cares?

4.12.71

	P	W	D	L	F	A	Pts
Man United	20	14	4	2	46	24	32
Derby County	20	10	7	3	35	16	27
Man City	20	11	5	4	37	20	27
Leeds United	20	12	3	5	30	17	27

4.3.72

	P	W	D	L	F	A	Pts
Man City	32	18	9	5	63	35	45
Leeds United	30	17	7	6	51	22	41
Derby County	30	16	8	6	52	29	40
Liverpool	31	16	7	8	44	27	39
Tottenham	31	14	10	7	48	32	38
Arsenal	30	16	5	9	44	29	37
Wolves	31	13	10	8	51	44	36
Sheffield Utd	30	14	7	9	51	44	35
Man United	30	14	7	9	52	45	35

UNITED IN SPACE

VOOM!

OFFICIAL MANCHESTER UNITED SUPPORTERS ROCKET

OLD TRAFFORD 2½ MILLION MILES — ALPHA CENTAURI 2½ MILLION MILES

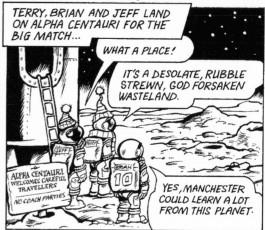

TERRY, BRIAN AND JEFF LAND ON ALPHA CENTAURI FOR THE BIG MATCH...

WHAT A PLACE!

IT'S A DESOLATE, RUBBLE STREWN, GOD FORSAKEN WASTELAND.

ALPHA CENTAURI WELCOMES CAREFUL TRAVELLERS

NO COACH PARTIES

YES, MANCHESTER COULD LEARN A LOT FROM THIS PLANET.

THIS IS THE BIG ONE TERRY. ALPHA CENTAURI AWAY.

YEAH, THEY'RE A GOOD SIDE ON THEIR DAY—WHICH UN--FORTUNATELY FOR US LASTS FOR 102 HOURS.

THESE DAYS THERE ARE NO EASY TIES.

PARTICULARLY NOT IN THE 'INTERGALACTIC CHAMPIONS' LEAGUE (WHICH NOW ACCEPTS RUNNERS UP IF THEY'RE FROM A BIG ENOUGH PLANET).

AND WITH US HOLDING A SLENDER 2-1 LEAD, WHAT WITH AWAY GOALS IN SPACE COUNTING DOUBLE.

SO TERRY, YOU HAVE GOT THE TICKETS, YEAH?

DON'T BE STUPID. WE DON'T NEED TICKETS. THIS STADIUM HOLDS TEN MILLION— ALTHOUGH IT WAS FIFTEEN MILLION BEFORE THE TAYLOR REPORT.

YOU MEAN WE'VE TRAVELLED TWENTY MILLION MILLION MILES AND WE HAVEN'T GOT ANY TICKETS?!!

YEAH, BUT WE'RE THE ONLY THREE TRAVELLING SUPPORTERS AREN'T WE? NONE OF THOSE BLOODY PART-TIMERS COULD BE BOTHERED.

GREAT! WE'LL HAVE THE AWAY STAND TO OURSELVES.

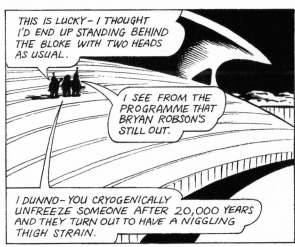

YOU HAVE TO QUESTION THE FORMAT OF THIS SEASON'S INTER-GALACTIC CHAMPIONS' LEAGUE (WHICH NOW ACCEPTS RUNNERS-UP IF THEY'RE FROM A BIG ENOUGH PLANET).

AND WE HAVEN'T EVEN REACHED THE KNOCKOUT STAGE YET.

WELL, IT'S A MARATHON NOT A SPRINT, BRIAN.

THE ALPHA CENTAURIANS ARE SOON ON THE ATTACK...

NOT SURE THIS PITCH SUITS OUR LADS - IT LOOKS A BIT FROZEN UNDERFOOT.

AND TENTACLE.

WELL, THEY ARE IN THE MIDDLE OF AN ICE-AGE HERE.

BOOT!

YES, THE RUBBLY SURFACE GIVES THE BUG-EYED TENTACLED LADS A DISTINCT ADVANTAGE.

THE CENTAURIANS SCORE!

THAT LEVELS THE TIE. TO THINK WE COULD HAVE STAYED AT HOME AND WATCHED THE GAME ON B SPACE B.

YEAH, BUT YOU DON'T GET THE ATMOSPHERE, DO YOU?

AND IT'S A DERBY DON'T FORGET.

Boot!

5-0. RIGHT LADS, I'M OFF.

BUT JEFF, THERE'S STILL 30 MINUTES TO GO.

YEAH, BUT I THOUGHT I'D TRY AND BEAT THE TRAFFIC.

TAP!

BOOMF!

SUDDENLY...

THE ALPHA CENTAURI STADIUM REGRETS TO ANNOUNCE THE MATCH HAS BEEN ABANDONED DUE TO FLOODLIGHT FAILURE.

DUE TO INTERGALACTIC POLICE REGULATIONS THE REARRANGED MATCH WILL TAKE PLACE IN TEN YEARS. ALL EXISTING TICKETS WILL STILL BE VALID...

BAH!

Leeds United	5	1	Manchester United

Jones 3, Clarke, Lorimer **45,399** **Burns**

1971–2 season – 19 February 1972

Don Revie's Leeds United side of the late 1960s and early 1970s used to grind out results with a winning combination of ruthless efficiency and cynicism. Occasionally, though, they would thump someone, and the Man United fixture came at just the right time. This was the sixth in a marvellous run of seven League defeats, during which they fell from 1st to 9th.

One consolation for Man United was that they did score their third League goal of the year.

Leeds United: Sprake, Madeley, Cooper, Bremner, Charlton, Hunter, Lorimer, Clarke, Jones, Giles, Gray
Manchester United: Stepney, O'Neill, Dunne, Burns, James, Sadler, Morgan, Kidd, Charlton, Gowling, Best

THE LEEDS LOCUSTS EAT THEIR FILL

OLD GRAY MAGIC

In a second half of ceaseless excitement Leeds annihilated Manchester United, reducing their frail defence to fumbling incompetence. As the cover in front of Stepney dissolved all five Leeds goals were tapped home from a few yards to emphasise the confusion caused by their incisive forwards. Gray's elusive dribbling and the thrust of Lorimer and Clarke so demoralised James and his backs that Jones was presented with three goals of bewildering simplicity.
Observer, 20 February 1972

REVIE: THIS WAS OUR GREATEST

Leeds United in the words of their manager Don Revie, turned on their greatest performance under his reign to crush Manchester United.

'I think our football in the second half was the best I have ever seen from the side,' declared Revie.
The *Sunday People*, 20 February 1972

TOP TEN SENDINGS-OFF

	PLAYER	MATCH	OFFENCE	COMMENT
10	**PAUL PARKER**	**v Queens Park Rangers, Premiership, 20 August 1994**	Professional foul on Les Ferdinand, who was through on goal. This happened just four minutes after Parker came on as substitute.	'Were the new laws applied like this everywhere else today?' **Alex Ferguson** (This was the first set of League fixtures where a sending off for a professional foul was mandatory.)
9	**PAT McGIBBON**	**v York City, Coca-Cola Cup 2nd round 1st leg, 20 September 1995**	Poleaxeing York centre-forward Paul Barnes just outside the area, and giving away a penalty, in the 3–0 home defeat. McGibbon never played for the first team again.	'I have no excuses.' **Alex Ferguson**
8	**MARK HUGHES**	**v Sheffield United, FA Cup 3rd round, 9 January 1994**	Aiming a kick from behind at David Tuttle, having already trampled on Chris Kamara in the first half. He later claimed he should have been protected by the referee.	'If referees are allowing Hughes to be used as some sort of punchbag because he is big and strong, then it's quite unfair.' **Alex Ferguson**
7	**PAUL INCE**	**v IFK Gothenburg, Champions League group A, 23 November 1994**	For hurling a barrage of expletives – somehow understood by the Italian referee – after a free kick had been awarded against him.	'You're a ******* ******, you ******* ****.' **Paul Ince**
6	**ERIC CANTONA**	**v Crystal Palace, Premiership, 25 January 1995**	For an off-the-ball kick at Richard Shaw – somewhat overshadowed by the off-the-pitch kick that followed seconds later.	'Off you go, Eric, it's an early bath for you.' **Matthew Simmons** (or so he claimed)

	PLAYER	MATCH	OFFENCE	COMMENT
5	**ROY KEANE**	**v Crystal Palace, FA Cup semi-final replay, 12 April 1995**	Stamping on Gareth Southgate and then stamping on him again as he lay on the ground, causing a mêlée between the players. Keane was seconds away from being substituted.	'It is important for football, particularly for the fans of Manchester United with their history and tradition, that they show their best behaviour both on and off the pitch.' **Alex Ferguson** to crowd before the match
4	**KEVIN MORAN**	**v Everton, FA Cup Final, 18 May 1985**	Scything down Peter Reid, who had a clear run on goal, and becoming the first player ever to be sent off in an FA Cup Final.	'All I could see was the ball. It wasn't as if the ball was gone and I took the player out.' **Alex Moran**
3	**PETER SCHMEICHEL**	**v Charlton Athletic, FA Cup quarter-final, 12 March 1994**	Two for the price of one. For handling the ball 40 yards from goal, then bringing down Charlton's Kim Grant in the process, with no defender in sight.	'He will be embarrassed if he sees it again.' **Alex Ferguson** referring to the referee, not Schmeichel
2	**ERIC CANTONA**	**v Swindon Town, Premiership, 19 March 1994**	For a vicious stamp on the prostrate John Moncur's chest, after the two players had tangled. Three days later, Cantona was sent off again against Arsenal.	'It is not something he premeditates. There is a spark in him that sometimes flares up. He knows that he has to behave himself and not take the law into his own hands.' **Alex Ferguson**
1	**OLE GUNNAR SOLSKJAER**	**v Newcastle United, Premiership, 18 April 1998**	At 1–1 a minute from time and the title disappearing, Robert Lee was bearing down on goal. Solskjaer – bizarrely the last defender – cynically chopped him down and walked off to a standing ovation for his 'selfless act'.	'Forward, isn't he? It was desperation. He's done it for all the right reasons in his mind.' **Alex Ferguson**

Manchester United	1	2	Bristol Rovers

McIlroy   29,349   Rudge, Bannister

League Cup 3rd round replay, 11 October 1972

United's ageing side, then propping up the First Division, found this time – as they did for most of that dismal season – that Old Trafford is never an easy place to get a result. Third Division Bristol Rovers could have won at the first attempt at Eastville, but they clearly fancied the extra gate revenue and allowed United to get the draw.

Man Utd: Stepney, Watson, Dunne, Young, James, Buchan, Morgan, Kidd (McIlroy), Charlton, Best, Moore
Bristol R: Sheppard, Roberts, Parsons, Prince, Taylor, Godfrey, Stephens, W. Jones, Rudge, Bannister, R. Jones

CRASH! UNITED OUT AS BEST FLUFFS PENALTY

BRAVE ROVERS HUMBLE UNITED

Trouble-torn Manchester United, bottom of the First Division, tumbled to further humiliation last night when they lost 2–1 to Third Divison Bristol Rovers in their League Cup third round replay at Old Trafford.

Rovers, who have already tasted giant-killing triumph this season with wins over Wolves and Sheffield United on their way to winning the Watney Cup, finally floored United with a Bruce Bannister header five minutes from time.

United, with Bobby Charlton having a miserable thirty-fifth birthday, could not complain.

They had a series of escapes before and after John Rudge had glanced Rovers ahead in half an hour.

They had a penalty after sixty-five minutes when Frankie Prince barged Ian Moore in the back and George Best, of all people, shot so tamely from the spot that Dick Sheppard saved with ease.

And they had what looked like an undeserved reprieve when substitute Sammy McIlroy levelled with a header nine minutes from the end.

The scoreline did hard-chasing Rovers scant justice. But, with five minutes left, they pulled out the winner they had merited, Bannister scoring with a brilliantly executed back header straight from a corner.

***Daily Mirror*, 12 October 1972**

UNITED IN EUROPE – 1

F.C. Porto	4	0	Manchester United

Duda 3, Oliveira   70,000

European Cup Winners' Cup 2nd round 1st leg, 19 October 1977

It almost made it worth United winning the FA Cup against Liverpool to see them go down in such an abject manner to the Portuguese Cup winners, FC Porto.

In the previous round, the United fans had attempted to get the club eliminated from the tournament after they ran riot in St Etienne. United were originally chucked out, but on appeal the club insisted that, if the team were to go out, it should be through their own inadequacies and not their fans'. They eventually got their wish. UEFA agreed that the 2nd leg of the St Etienne tie could take place in Plymouth, not realising that this actually reduced the journey for most of the United fans.

In the return leg against Porto, Manchester United scored five times, which makes it all the more amusing that the Portuguese side scored two, and knocked United out of the competition.

FC Porto: Fonseca, Gabriel, Simoes, Freitas, Murca, Teixeira, Rodolfo, Octavio, Duda, Oliveira, Seninho
Man Utd: Stepney, Nicholl, Albiston, McIlroy, Houston (Forsyth), Buchan, McGrath, McCreery, Coppell, Macari, Hill

OH, YOU REDS!

United, the bright young flower of English football, were ground underfoot in Portugal.

Striker Duda destroyed them with a hat-trick in yet another match that emphasised how far behind the rest of the world most of English football has fallen.

United are one of our better teams in terms of technique and enterprise but last night they were little boys lost in a man's world.

Oporto were so superior in the craft of the game that United could not have complained if they had doubled their score.

The Portuguese were streets ahead in control, passing and finishing.
The Sun, 20 October 1977

UNITED ROCKED BY PORTO GOAL BLAST

Manchester United flew home from Portugal early this morning with their pride and their dreams of conquering Europe shattered, after being soundly thrashed by FC Porto, in the first leg of an unexpectedly one-sided Cup Winners' Cup tie.

MONEY WELL SPENT 1

VIV ANDERSON

BEFORE

Tireless, overlapping right-back and veteran of over 300 matches for Nottingham Forest. Also performed with distinction for Arsenal and England.

GARRY BIRTLES

BEFORE

Willowy, free-scoring striker proved a bargain buy for Forest from non-League Long Eaton United, bagging a hatful of crucial goals when it mattered most.

GARTH CROOKS

BEFORE

Lethal raider for Stoke and Tottenham, with a quick turn of pace and a sharp finish, he scored 48 League goals for each of these clubs.

LAURIE CUNNINGHAM

BEFORE

Pacy flankman with an eye for goal, who earned England call-ups while on the paid ranks of both West Brom and Real Madrid.

PETER BARNES

BEFORE

Speedy winger, with superb crossing ability and a sizzling shot. First capped soon after joining the paid ranks at the age of 20.

ALAN BRAZIL

BEFORE

Scored 70 goals in 154 games for Ipswich. There's been no better player at holding up the ball, or more decisive in the box with his crisp finishing.

JORDI CRUYFF

BEFORE

Stylish midfielder who can scheme or score and whose elevation to the Barcelona side had nothing to do with the fact that his father was manager. Dutch caps.

PETER DAVENPORT

BEFORE

Captured from Cammell Laird shipyard. Adroit spearhead, with an instinctive feel for where the goal is.

MONEY WELL SPENT 1

VIV ANDERSON

AFTER
Tired, over-the-hill right-back and a true veteran. Broke the domestic transfer record for a player over 30 when signed from the Gunners for £250,000.

GARRY BIRTLES

AFTER
Willowy, barn-door-missing striker proved a bargain sale for Forest at £1.25 million and a bargain buy when they bought him back for one-fifth of that figure.

GARTH CROOKS

AFTER
Failed to score on his bow against Watford, and only found the net twice for United, his raiding proving less than lethal.

LAURIE CUNNINGHAM

AFTER
Secured by United as temporary replacement for Steve Coppell, he made the No. 11 shirt his own, when he later joined Marseille.

PETER BARNES

AFTER
Had left Manchester City and his Maine Road form by the time he joined United in 1985, bagging just 2 goals in 20 games.

ALAN BRAZIL

AFTER
Scored eight goals in 30 matches for United. There's been no better player at holding back his team, with his indecision in the box and soggy finishing.

JORDI CRUYFF

AFTER
Would have benefited in his time at Old Trafford if Alex Ferguson had been his Dad. Not many more Dutch caps.

PETER DAVENPORT

AFTER
Some 22 goals in 35 matches is a fine return for a striker – unfortunately, Davenport played 92 times. Fans' solution was to send him back to Cammell Laird shipyard.

Stand Up If You Hate Newton Heath

Part One

It was Saturday, the day of the big match. Newton Heath were playing host to their distant rivals Burnley. Ernest Dobbins kissed his lady wife on the cheek, and gave each of his nine children a firm but not too familiar handshake, as he prepared to take his leave.

'Well Augusta dearest, I'm off to the association football,' he reminded her. 'This being 1893, and travel still being arduous, I may be late back tonight – like Tuesday.'

'I understand, Ernest dear, as the ground is over three miles away. Please remember the children fondly, as they may not all be alive when you return home, because it is indeed 1893 and modern medicine isn't what it will be.'

Behind them, there was a gentle thud, as little Charlotte fell to the unforgiving stone floor.

'There, what did I tell you. Now you will endeavour to be back for the funeral, won't you?'

'Indeed I shall, madam.' With those words, he grabbed his finest stovepipe hat, closed the front door and headed out into the morning mist, contemplating his four-hour peregrination to the ground.

At that moment, a brougham was passing. A yellow candle flickered at the front, indicating that it was for hire. If only I could afford to travel by cab, he thought, it would cut down my journey by at least ten minutes. Then he remembered that he was a child light, and thus the cab fare was now within

his means. So poor little Charlotte had not given her life in vain after all.

'Cab!' he shouted, and clambered aboard.

'You off to t'match, sir?'

'Yes. How the deuce did you know?'

'The Newton Heath cravat round tha' neck was a clue, sir – not to mention the words, "Play up Newton Heath" inscribed on tha' stovepipe hat. So who are the Heathens playing?'

'Burnley.'

'Oh, Burnley, sir,' said the cabbie, wisely. 'They're a good side in these days, although I do predict lean times ahead in about a century.'

'Indeed, the Clarets are a tough nut to crack,' admitted Ernest. 'I hear they play a very defensive 2–1–7 formation, so it's unlikely we'll see more than ten or eleven goals this afternoon.'

'That's why I gave up going, sir. I mean, football's not what it used to be in't old days ...'

'I thought these were the old days,' muttered Ernest under his massive beard.

'... My wife and I prefer watching sphairistiké now, or tennis as it will probably soon be called,' continued the cabbie, oblivious to Ernest's interjection. 'I used to attend regular, but then I began to notice that most of t'Newton Heath supporters came from all round t'country – places like Altrincham and Stockport. Some travelled from as far away as Oldham sir!'

Ernest took a pinch of snuff from his

official Newton Heath snuffbox and looked out of the mud-spattered window, trying his best to ignore the opinions of the cabman.

'Then there's all those foreign players, sir,' he continued. 'Just what do they bring to t'game, that's what I'd like to know. Last I heard Newton Heath had two Scotchmen and a Welshman in their team! I mean it's all right when t'weather's nice at start of t'season, but come February they'll wish they were back in Abergavenny or Third Lanark.'

The cabbie continued in this vein for another two hours, but Ernest had ceased to listen. His mind wandered to thoughts of his eight dear children – and how many more of them would have to die before he could afford a season ticket. Two? Three? He stroked his even bigger beard. After all, there was a diphtheria epidemic in the next street …

At this moment these gay reflections were brought to an end when he realised he had at last achieved his destination. The proud stadium that was the envy of all football, and would surely be the home of Newton Heath for ever more – North Road, Newton.

Ernest handed over a farthing to the cabbie. 'Haven't you got anything smaller?' the man growled.

'There isn't anything smaller,' said Ernest.

'Oh, so there isn't,' said the cabbie, and drove off, chuckling to himself mysteriously.

As he stood on the kerbside, Ernest looked around him and had a sense of foreboding. Something wasn't quite right. Where was everybody? Either he was too early, or the diphtheria epidemic had spread further than he'd thought. He looked at his fob watch and saw to his horror that there was less than half an hour until kick-off …

EXCUSES 1

Q. What was one of the reasons given for Manchester United sacking chef James Allison in 1992?

A. He cut tomatoes into the wrong shape. When preparing tomatoes for salads for patrons of executive boxes, he wilfully and persistently sliced the said fruit (not vegetable) into quarters. His superiors had previously told him to cut them into posh feathery shapes. He wrote to chairman Martin Edwards, who never replied – perhaps he was too busy tucking into those posh feathery-shaped tomatoes.

Q. Why did the British government cause Man United to suffer two successive 4–0 defeats, against Porto and West Brom, in October 1977?

A. The team were suffering the after-effects of cholera jabs needed for a goodwill trip to Iran. The injections had been administered ten days before the Middle East trip, after which Jimmy Greenhoff and Arthur Albiston became ill and had to miss the two 4–0 pastings. Luckily, they were all better in time for the trip to Tehran. The defeat at West Brom was also attributed to a flight in the middle of the night back from Portugal, after their tie with Porto had finished at 12.30 a.m. There's no truth in the rumour that the game actually kicked off at 7.30 p.m. and the referee added 3½ hours of stoppage to see if United could score four.

DRUBBINGS — 2

Crystal Palace	5	0	Manchester United

Mulligan 2, Rogers 2, Whittle   39,484

1972–3 season – 16 December 1972

The previous Saturday, Man United had lost 2–0 at home to Stoke City to go third from bottom. George Best was on one of his walkabouts and was missing, presumed drunk in a London nightclub. Louis Edwards, meanwhile, was giving his full backing to Best and no backing at all to manager Frank O'Farrell. Then came the match with fellow-strugglers Crystal Palace.

Crystal Palace: Jackson, Mulligan, Bell, Blyth, Taylor, Phillip, Payne, Cooke, Hughes, Whittle, Rogers
Manchester United: Stepney, O'Neill, Sadler, Buchan, Dunne (Law), Young, Morgan, Kidd, MacDougall, Davies, Moore.

THE DAY UNITED BIT THE DUST

To put it in the words of Palace life-president Arthur Wait, 'I never thought I'd live to see the day we'd beat Manchester United so convincingly. They were the worst United side I've ever seen.'

Until United forget what they are going to do, or not do, with George Best, and concentrate on sorting out the rest of their problems, they are going to blunder from disaster to disaster. As one would expect, Palace had heroes galore. Skipper Mulligan hit two goals, wizard winger Rogers also hit two, and £100,000 new boy Whittle scored a fine debut goal. But the man who stood out was Phillip, a tireless midfield worker who showed all the attributes United so sadly lack.

The Sunday People, 17 December 1972

ROGERS SHATTERS A SAD UNITED

UNITED FOR SALE

PART 1

ROBERT MAXWELL

IN NOVEMBER 1983 MANCHESTER UNITED WERE HUMBLED BY LITTLE OXFORD IN THE MILK CUP...

I FEEL EVER SO HUMBLE.

SO DO I.

TAP!

OXFORD'S LOYAL CHAIRMAN, THE SELF EFFACING ROBERT MAXWELL MADE HIS USUAL APPEARANCE...

I'M HERE NOW— YOU CAN STOP WATCHING THAT. I'M THE SELF EFFACING ROBERT MAXWELL. **GIVE US AN R...**

NOW, MINION— WHICH OF THESE TEAMS AM I CHAIRMAN OF AGAIN?

ERM— O-OXFORD UNITED MR. M-M-MAXWELL, SIR.

RIDICULOUS! A MAN LIKE ME SHOULD BE CHAIRMAN OF MANCHESTER UNITED.

I'LL SEE WHAT I CAN DO, SIR.

6 WEEKS LATER...

MORNING, MR. EDWARDS SIR. YOU'RE HERE NICE AND EARLY.

YES, I'VE GOT A SECRET MEETING WITH ROBERT MAXWELL.

I KNOW, I READ ABOUT IT IN THE PAPER THIS MORNING.

AT A SECRET LOCATION...

MANCHESTER UNITED WELCOMES ROBERT MAXWELL TO HIS HUSH HUSH TALKS HERE AT OLD TRAFFORD

THIS LOOKS DISCREET ENOUGH EDWARDS, NOW LET'S GET STRAIGHT TO BUSINESS!

NAME YOUR PRICE AND I'LL PAY IT!

TWENTY MILLION!

NOW NAME A SMALLER PRICE.

OK, I'LL WRITE A FIGURE ON A PIECE OF PAPER AND SEE HOW THAT GRABS YOU.

I'LL HAVE TO CONSULT MY PENSION FUNDS – THAT'S TO SAY MY BANK BALANCE TO SEE IF THIS IS VIABLE.

EDWARDS, I WANT THIS CLUB. I'VE ALWAYS BEEN A FAN OF MANCHESTER UNITED.

ISN'T THAT WHAT YOU TOLD BIRMINGHAM CITY LAST MONTH?

NO, I TOLD THEM I'D ALWAYS BEEN A FAN OF BIRMINGHAM CITY. NOW GOOD DAY TO YOU.

Touchline™

Are you sick of watching the live United match on your own every Sunday? Is there nobody there to help you carry your bags when you stagger out of your local United superstore? Then it's high time you thought of joining TOUCHLINE™, the Manchester United dating agency.

With over 25 million United fans between the ages of one and 65, you'd think it was as easy as a home game against Barnsley to find the partner of your dreams. But as 24 million of you never have the opportunity to visit the Theatre of Dreams ® ™ ©, you never have a chance to meet. That is, until now!

TOUCHLINE™ is exclusive to Manchester United supporters, and it could be the best £249.99 you'll ever spend, outside the United shop. Soon you could be walking hand in hand through the streets of Lincoln. Or maybe one day you could actually afford to come to Old Trafford and see the perfect match with <u>your</u> perfect match.

Who knows, you may eventually marry and have children – and the good news is they'll almost certainly grow up to be Manchester United fans. Now all you have to do is fill in this simple questionnaire and send it together with your cheque to the following address:

TOUCHLINE™
PO Box 5063, Godalming, Surrey

TICK ANY BOX WHICH APPLIES

PERSONAL INFORMATION
❏ Mr
❏ Mrs
❏ Miss
❏ Ms
❏ Herr
❏ Frau
❏ Señor
❏ Señorita
❏ Sahib
❏ Memsahib
❏ Dom
❏ Bruce
❏ Sheila

Surname ....
First name ....
Address ....
....
....
....
....

MARITAL STATUS
❏ Single
❏ Divorced
❏ Widowed
❏ Desperate
❏ Don't know

YOUR IDEAL PARTNER
❏ Single
❏ Divorced
❏ Widowed
❏ The physiotherapist's wife

YOUR BUILD
❏ Large
❏ Medium
❏ Small
❏ Paul Scholes

EARNINGS
❏ Low income
❏ Middle income
❏ Rich beyond the dreams of avarice
❏ Season-ticket holder

YOUR INTERESTS
❏ Football
❏ Football since 1993
❏ Timekeeping
❏ Kung-fu
❏ Star-gazing
❏ Mirror-gazing
❏ Wining
❏ Whining
❏ Bleating
❏ Paranormal
❏ Paranoia

HOW WOULD YOU DESCRIBE YOURSELF?
❏ Loyal
❏ Fervent
❏ Fairweather
❏ Off to the car-park as soon as one goal goes in

ATTRACTIVENESS
Would you say you are:
❏ Very attractive
❏ Quite attractive
❏ Average
❏ Pug ugly
❏ Gary Neville

AGE OF IDEAL PARTNER
❏ 51–65
❏ 36–50
❏ 26–35
❏ 16–25
❏ Ole Gunnar Solskjaer

DISLIKES
❏ Liverpool
❏ Unnecessary criticism
❏ Any criticism
❏ Penalty shootouts
❏ Kenny Dalglish
❏ Unbiased referees
❏ Mancunians
❏ Southampton away
❏ Any criticism whatsoever

HOPES AND DREAMS
❏ Happy marriage
❏ Good job
❏ Steady income
❏ Champions' League win
❏ Meeting Jimmy Hill down a dark alley

DRUBBINGS – 3

West Bromwich Albion	4	0	Manchester United

Giles, A. Brown, Cantello, Treacy   38,037

1976–7 season – 16 October 1976

West Bromwich Albion	4	0	Manchester United

Cross 2, Wile, Cunningham   27,649

1977–8 season – 22 October 1977

Forget Liverpool, Leeds or Arsenal. The team Man United feared most in the late 70s was West Bromwich Albion, particularly if it happened to be late October. Prior to the 1976 defeat, United had finished their previous League match sitting on top of the table. They walked off the pitch at the Hawthorns in the slightly less prestigious eighth spot.

The match in October 1977 started a run of four successive defeats that effectively scuppered United's League season.

They thought they'd laid the Albion bogey the following season, when they put three past West Brom at Old Trafford – the only trouble was the Baggies scored five themselves. By the end of the decade, United were obviously coming to terms with the October Hawthorns hoodoo – in 1979, they came away with a creditable 2–0 hammering.

16.10.76
West Bromwich Albion: Osborne, Mulligan, Cantello, T.Brown, Wile, Robertson, Martin, Treacy, A.Brown, Giles, Johnston
Man Utd: Stepney, Nicholl, Houston, Daly, Greenhoff, Waldron, Coppell, McIlroy, Pearson, Macari (McCreery), Hill

22.10.77
West Bromwich Albion: Godden, Mulligan, Statham, Brown, Wile, Robertson, Cantello, Cunningham, Cross, Robson, Johnston
Man Utd: Stepney, Forsyth, Rogers, McIlroy, Nicholl, Buchan, Coppell, McCreery (McGrath), Pearson, Macari, Hill

UNITED LAID LOW AGAIN

FRANK O'FARRELL

1971–2

In June 1971, Sir Matt Busby decided once again to retire as manager, only this time he promised to give up all managerial posts and take his place on the United board. Celtic boss Jock Stein was number one choice and looked like he was about to take over, until the moment that he spoke to Sir Matt and realised that his fellow Scot even now wasn't ready to let go.

The man eventually chosen was Frank O'Farrell, who'd done a sterling job at Torquay United and had just steered Leicester City into the First Division. He was a popular choice with the players. As an outsider and a disciplinarian, O'Farrell clearly wouldn't be swayed by cliques and factions that operated in the club, and wouldn't be afraid to drop or sell a player just because he'd won a European Cup medal.

If Wilf McGuinness discovered that being an insider didn't help, Frank O'Farrell found that being an outsider was no better. The established players, the Busby influence, and the so-called United tradition were all as powerful as ever. Even at the end of his tenure, there were still seven members of the European Cup winning side who were regulars in the first team.

His honeymoon period lasted four months. At the end of 1971, United were clear at the top of the League. During 1972, O'Farrell presided over no less than 23 League defeats and just ten victories. Impressive though that record is, it doesn't tell the whole story. He was considered aloof and uncommunicative by the players. The players he chose to strengthen the squad – such as Ted MacDougall, Ian Storey-Moore and Wyn Davies – were either not up to the job, injury prone or already past it. But what finished him off was George Best.

Best was spotted more often in London nightclubs than at the training ground. His lenient treatment was causing resentment among the players and eventually O'Farrell decided to act. At the beginning of December 1972, Best was dropped and put on the transfer list. A week later, without consulting O'Farrell, Busby and chairman Louis Edwards took him off the list. United lost their next match to relegation rivals Crystal Palace by a magnificent 5–0. The board now had all the excuse they needed. Three days later, O'Farrell was gone.

Louis Edwards' attempt to sack his manager almost foundered because O'Farrell said he was too busy to turn up to the Edwards meat plant, where the entire United board had gathered. Curiously enough, the next day, he wasn't busy at all. The final irony – given that his attempt to get tough with George Best had contributed to his downfall – was that Best was shown the door by United on the same day he was.

The United board hadn't been so insensitive as to sack O'Farrell just after Christmas. They sacked him just before Christmas instead. Merry Christmas, Frank.

By November 1973, O'Farrell was back in work – as manager of Cardiff City. Five months later, he was privileged enough to be appointed manager of Iran. By 1976, there was only one job that could lure him back to Blighty – a second spell at his beloved Torquay United. He returned for a third spell in 1981, before settling into retirement in the town.

**'He came as a stranger and left as a stranger.'
DENIS LAW**

UNITED CRISIS

BOOTED OUT

BEST AND O'FARRELL SACKED IN SHOCK SOCCER PURGE

In Britain's most sensational Soccer purge, Manchester United idol George Best was sacked yesterday – along with three top club officials including manager Frank O'Farrell.
Daily Mirror, **20 December 1972**

CHAMPIONSHIP FLOPS

NUMBER TWO

1973-1974

The 1973–4 season was the time that made all those years of despising Manchester United worthwhile, when all our dreams came true, when our lives became complete. It was the *seasonus mirabilis*, the icing on the cake, the cherry on the icing on the cake, it was the best of times, it was the even better of times. Seasons just don't come any better than this. In three words: United were relegated.

In the previous season, United had been stuck in the relegation zone for much of the season and had been lucky to escape. Surely they couldn't get any worse. Oh yes they could. Tommy Docherty succeeded in dismantling this ageing side, whose glories were now long behind them. Law and Charlton had both gone, and so had Best – usually to a London nightclub or Marbella.

Fortunately, Docherty neglected to replace them with anyone who was any good. The first match – a 3–0 defeat at Arsenal – set the tone for the season. Defeat followed defeat, humiliation followed humiliation. The only person who could look back on the first half of the season with pride was goalkeeper Alex Stepney. He covered up many of the howlers of the Man United defence, and was also sitting proudly on top of the goalscorers' charts – with two.

In December, George Best joined Stepney as equal top scorer, but it was to be his last goal for United. The season before, he had threatened to jump ship if the team was relegated, and for once he was true to his word. After the traditional New Year's Day thumping by

QPR, he staggered off to drown his sorrows, as only George knew how. He never played for Manchester United again.

Surprisingly, it wasn't until the New Year that they settled into the relegation zone, and, once there, they never left it. A brief revival in April gave the fans some pointless hope and the rest of us a few jitters. But they were only delaying the inevitable.

It was 4.35 p.m. on Saturday 27 April 1974 when the great moment finally came. United needed a draw at home to Manchester City to have any chance of escaping the drop. With eight minutes to go, the match was still goalless. The ball somehow bobbled through to the discarded former United hero Denis Law, who almost apologetically backheeled the ball into the net. United fans invaded the pitch in a bid to get the match abandoned. They succeeded but the result stood, and all they had done was prevent their side having any opportunity to get an equaliser. Let's just say it again: Manchester United were relegated.

	Goals
McIlroy	6
Macari	5
McCalliog	4
Greenhoff	3
Stepney	2
Best	2

DOC BOTTOM!

	P	W	D	L	F	A	Pts
West Ham	29	7	9	13	33	44	23
Birmingham	27	5	9	13	29	47	19
Norwich City	28	4	10	14	22	41	18
Man United	27	5	7	15	22	36	17

UNITED DOWN!

Final Table	P	W	D	L	F	A	Pts
Birmingham	42	12	13	17	33	44	23
Southampton	42	11	14	17	47	68	36
Man United	42	10	12	20	38	48	32
Norwich City	42	7	15	20	37	62	29

MARK BOSNICH

(1989–91) – Three games between the sticks for the Aussie before he went off to 'do' Europe.

TOMMY JACKSON

(1975–7) – Known as Everton and Forest player but 19 games for United seemed to pass without incident.

BILLY GARTON

(1984–8) – Never-present defender, who managed just 41 matches in five seasons.

STEVE JAMES

(1968–75) – In 129 matches, he still failed to imprint himself on anyone's memory banks – even his family are rumoured to have beenunaware that he played for United.

LEE MARTIN

(1988–94) – The least memorable Cup Final winner of all time, scored in 1990, by the least memorable Cup Final winner of all time.

PETER BARNES

(1985–6) – Made his reputation at City, improved it at West Brom, lost it at United, in just 20 games.

GEORGE GRAHAM

(1973–4) – Had huge influence in short time at United – soon they were strolling down to Division Two.

GIULIANO MAIORANA

(1989) – The one-time future of football managed seven games for United but wasn't good enough to play for anyone else at league level

LAURIE CUNNINGHAM

(1983) – Signed on loan from Real Madrid, scoring more goals in his five matches than Garry Birtles once managed in a whole season – one.

RON DAVIES

(1974–5) – Before he joined United, he'd scored 276 League goals. By the time he left, he'd scored 276 goals – after eight appearances, all as substitute.

GARTH CROOKS

(1983–4) – Proved that he was very far from the answer to all of Big Ron's goalscoring problems, with a ratio of a goal every three-and-a-half games – making a total of two.

It's better to have played for United and lost than never to have played for United at all. These players somehow managed to pull on a United shirt without most of us noticing.

Sub TOMMY BALDWIN

Baldwin (1975) – United was just a two-match stop for this prolific striker on the journey from Chelsea to Gravesend & Northfleet.

Manager WILF McGUINNESS

Who?

Southampton	1	0	Manchester United

Stokes   100,000

FA Cup Final, 1 May 1976

In one of the greatest and most pleasing Cup Final upsets, Southampton – who finished 6th in the Second Division that season – turned over United. Tommy Docherty was so complacent that it's a surprise he didn't insist the trophy was sent to the engravers before the match.

When the semi-final draw pitted United against then-champions Derby County at Hillsborough, leaving Southampton to play Third Division Crystal Palace to decide the other FA Cup Final place, Docherty dismissed the last two teams with the words, 'This is the first time that the Cup Final will be played at Hillsborough. The other semi-final is a bit of a joke really.'

In a quote Alex Ferguson would have been proud of, Docherty – no wiser after the event than before – bleated, 'We lost because they scored so late in the match. I'd much have preferred to get an early goal and we would then have got right into it.' So basically if United had scored and Southampton hadn't, then United would have won.

Southampton: Turner, Rodrigues, Peach, Holmes, Blyth, Steele, Gilchrist, Channon, Osgood, McCalliog, Stokes,
Manchester Utd: Stepney, Forsyth, Houston, Daly, Greenhoff, Buchan, Coppell, McIlroy, Pearson, Macari, Hill (McCreery)

SOUTHAMPTON CLIP UNITED'S WINGS

Against all logic and prediction, the unexpected happened once more in the FA Cup Final on Saturday. On a sunny May Day it was Southampton, the supposed underdogs, who danced around the maypole and around vaunted Manchester United to win the trophy for the first time in their history. They gained it worthily with a single goal by Stokes seven minutes from full time, to become the second Division 2 side in four seasons to upset the odds. It was no fluke. They had done their homework.

Geoffrey Green, *The Times* **3 May 1976**

SOUTHAMPTON'S TRIUMPH IS A TONIC FOR SOCCER BACKWATERS

As convoys of jubilant supporters drove home along the M3 on Saturday evening – their cars, mini-buses and coaches festooned with scarves, rosettes and banners – every motorway bridge was manned by kindred spirits saluting the good news from Wembley.

Though there will be much weeping and gnashing of teeth in scores of Manchester United supporters' clubs, this turn up for the book can only be good for the game.

24 ½ HOUR MAN U-TV

FULL GLOBAL COVERAGE THROUGHOUT THE WORLD*

6.00 Wake Up With Beck And Posh
Three hours of Britain's favourite couple staring into each other's eyes as soon as the cameras are on them.

9.00 Thought For The Day, with Andy Cole.
What will Andy's thought be on this particular day?

10.00 Why I Support United.
Zoe Ball explains why she became a Manchester United supporter on the day after they won the Championship in 1993.

11.00 Wilf McGuinness: A Tribute
An in-depth appreciation of the contribution made by one of Manchester's greatest-ever managers.

11.01 Live And Kicking
A look back on some of Roy Keane's best-loved fouls and sendings-off.

11.30 The Big Match
Manchester United Youth Team versus Grimsby Town under-21s. Live non-stop action from the United training ground, pitch B.
(In the event of excessive injury time being necessary, subsequent programme times may vary.)

1.30 The Big Match* (r)
Manchester United Youth Team versus Grimsby Town under-21s. Live non-stop action from the United training ground, pitch B.
Another chance to see this potential humdinger.

3.30 Red Dwarf
Pint-sized frolics, starring Paul Scholes.

4.00 Win, Draw Or Moan
Gloomy timekeeping quiz, with Alex Ferguson

4.30 Countdown
Gloomy timekeeping quiz, with Alex Ferguson. With delectable sidekick Brian Kidd.
(In the event of extra questions being necessary, subsequent programme times may vary.)

5.00 Rainbow
Red and yellow and pink and green, orange and purple and blue. A history of some of the Manchester United kits of the past 12 months.

5.15 The Money Programme
Non-stop profit-making and excessive price increases from the United accounts office.

6.00 Football Special
A preview of some of the A team's upcoming matches against Everton A, Sizewell B, Mel B, Special K and Henry V.

7.00 Red Nose Day
Peter Schmeichel shouts about some of his favourite moments from Danish comedy.

7.30 Can't Play Won't Play
Ralph Milne tries to explain away his performances in a United shirt.

8.00 The Pallisters
Timeless, creaky-kneed drama.

8.45 The Kevin Moran Hour
A lively mixture of comedy, light-hearted chat and bloodied head wounds.
(In the event of programme not lasting the distance, subsequent programmes may be screened sooner than scheduled.)

9.45 What The Papers Say
Alex Ferguson slags off the day's papers, rooting out any hidden criticism, while Nicky Butt just looks at the photographs.

10.00 God's Gift
David Beckham talks about the importance of looking good and takes a fond look in the mirror.

10.30 There's Lovely
Ryan Giggs reminisces on all his performances in Wales friendlies and then desperately tries to pad out the remaining 25 minutes.

11.00 Late Night Horror
Highlights of recent matches against Southampton from The Dell.

12.00 The Late Late Show
Tackling masterclass with Roy Keane.

1.00–6.30 (Something In Norwegian)
Ronnie Johnsen, Ole Gunnar Solskjaer and Henning Berg discuss burning issues of concern to all of us, in their native Norwegian.

* Not available in Manchester, England

46

Arsenal	3	2	Manchester United

Talbot, Stapleton, Sunderland   100,000   McQueen, McIlroy

FA Cup Final, 12 May 1979

This is a Cup Final that, with five minutes to go, was heading for a rather dull 2–0 win to Arsenal, yet would still have found a place in our hearts, if only for the score and United's lacklustre performance. What makes it so wonderful, however, is that United were given hope when they scored in the 86th and 88th minutes to equalise, only to have that hope so gloriously dashed less than a minute later. For those 55 seconds, the United fans must have believed the match would be remembered only for their comeback, and that the game would be theirs for the taking in extra time.

Steve Coppell certainly filled his 55 seconds. 'At 2–2 my imagination ran riot. I was so convinced we were going to win, I could even see the headlines in the Sunday newspapers. The score would be 4–2. It was inevitable.'

Perhaps if he'd spent less time riotously imagining and score forecasting, and more time doing that tracking back he was so famous for, Coppell might have noticed Liam Brady making a 30 yard run down the left. A pass to Graham Rix, a cross to Alan Sunderland and the most memorable FA Cup Final of modern times was complete – and Steve Coppell's Sunday newspapers had to be rewritten.

Arsenal: Jennings, Rice, Nelson, Talbot, O'Leary, Young, Brady, Sunderland, Stapleton, Price (Walford), Rix
Man Utd: Bailey, Nicholl, Albiston, McIlroy, McQueen, Buchan, Coppell, J. Greenhoff, Jordan, Macari, Thomas

HAS THERE EVER BEEN A FINAL LIKE THIS!

Last season was the most exciting ever. At one time it looked like Arsenal then it looked like Chelsea – but in the end after they won five games in a row, I decided to be a Manchester United fan. It's brilliant. We win all the time. Not like my Dad's team. Norwich City are rubbish. Boo! We hate Norwich. I hope one day United will play at Norwich in the FA Cup and then I will get to see my team, and United will win and Dad will look silly.

Sometimes I hate my Mum and Dad. They said I could have a new Man United strip for Christmas, they said I could have a new Man United strip for my birthday, but that's so unfair. That's only twice a year. What about all the other strips? Timothy Andrews' Mum – 'cos he hasn't got a Dad – bought him the Champion's league away kit last week. I want one. And I want the Champion's league second choice home kit too. That'll show everybody I support Man United just as much as Timothy Andrews. More.

Timothy Andrews' Mum buys him everything. He's got loads of United things – a scarf, a hat, two mugs, posters, a piggy bank and a mobile phone. He also has his own front door key on a Manchester United key ring, which he needs because when his Mum comes home from work she gets his tea and then she has to go out to work again.

Timothy Andrews' bedroom's not as good as mine. I've got brilliant pictures all over the walls and my wardrobe, all the way up to the ceiling, and I had to stand on a chair. I've got 138 pictures of Ryan Giggs who is my favourite at the moment, and 83 pictures of David Beckham who might soon be my favourite, and 32 pictures of Peter Schmeichel and 25 pictures of Ole Gunner ~~Sokjer~~ ~~Solksjar~~ Solskjer and 1 picture of Kevin Pilkington by mistake.

Another thing I don't like about my Dad is that he teases me. He says that Man United used to never win and that Liverpool used to be always the best. But that can't be true. And Dad says I should support Norwich City because they're the nearest team to our house. But that's stupid. They're not even good. Sometimes I wonder if he really is my Dad.

In my class Manchester United are the favourite team, but I still talk to the people who like Arsenal, Chelsea and Newcastle. We all gang up on Robert Smedley who likes Norwich. Even Matthew Kirk can join in. He supports Blackburn, though I don't know why. I don't think he can remember.

Another thing I don't like about my Dad is that he bought me the wrong boots. I asked Mum and Dad for proper Ryan Giggs Reebok and he got me some unofficial Ryan Giggs gym shoes. I wish I had a Dad like Timothy Andrews' Mum.

MUFC

LOUIS EDWARDS

In January 1980, Cheshire butcher Louis Edwards was the subject of a *World In Action* special on ITV, when the programme made a number of serious allegations about his business practices. Edwards, the jolly-faced, cleaver-wielding chairman of Manchester United Football Club since 1965, was accused of gaining a majority shareholding by irregular means and of profiting substantially from these dealings.

The documentary, entitled 'The Man Who Bought United', alleged that United had induced promising schoolchildren to join the club using a secret cash fund imaginatively codenamed 'No. 2 Account'. It also suggested that Edwards, whose firm specialised in supplying meat to schools, had sent free produce to those people who could secure him school-meal contracts.

The story was front-page news and the Trade Secretary, John Nott, was asked by Manchester MPs to authorise an inquiry into the club's financial affairs. Thirty-two leading shareholders requested that Edwards step down as chairman until police investigations into the allegations were completed. They never were, as less than a month after the programme was shown, Louis Edwards was dead following a heart attack in his bath. All inquiries ended with his death.

What *World In Action* didn't say, perhaps because Louis Edwards was then still alive, is that his firm had sold poor-quality meat to schools. A Manchester Council report as long ago as 1966 had made the accusation, 12 years before the company was finally fined under the Food And Drugs Act for selling low-quality, fatty meat.

The other occasion that Edwards's meat firm made the papers was when – like a Mancunian version of The Long Good Friday – it was used as the setting for the dismissal of manager Frank O'Farrell. He was not the first or last person to be afraid of getting the chop there.

MARTIN EDWARDS

With the passing of Louis Edwards, the football world held its collective breath. Who would be the new chairman of Manchester United? Would it be Sir Matt Busby – the esteemed elder statesman who'd masterminded United's on-field triumphs and transformed the club into a legend? Or would it be young Martin, the beanpole butcher's boy blessed with a more eminent qualification – the surname Edwards? On 22 March 1980, they got their answer when Martin Edwards was elected unopposed and became the youngest chairman in the League after a certain Elton John.

Martin Edwards had first been welcomed into that holiest of holies – the United boardroom – at the tender age of 24, when his dad had recommended he become a director of the club. For the next ten years he sat at the back and didn't say very much. In the meantime, he also worked a bit – learning the ropes in the family firm and doing some consulting jobs for Argyll Foods. In addition to his lofty position at United, in summer 1980 he became a non-executive director of Exclusive Cleaning and Maintenance Ltd, a firm owned by rent-a-mouth, Tory MP-to-be David Evans. Edwards received commission for any new work contracts he generated until 1985.

THE EDWARDS FAMILY

Edwards first got a chance to flex his new-found muscle at United in November 1981, when along with other chairmen he voted for the FA's rules to be changed to permit one paid director per club. The following month the United board appointed their first full-time executive – a chap by the name of Martin Edwards. By August 1982, only four United players were earning more than the £40,000 per annum he was making.

At the United AGM in November 1984, Martin Edwards – thanks to new FA rules concerning the limits on share dividend payouts – trousered some £77,000. The next year it was decreed that half this annual bonus would be accounted for by including one per cent of profit on transfers. Naturally enough, this caused an outcry among the United faithful, as it gave the appearance that Edwards had more of an interest in selling players rather than buying them, and it was hastily shelved.

Throughout the 1980s, United may have been falling short on the pitch but in the boardroom Edwards was for ever dreaming up new money-making ventures. In 1982, the club formed an unlikely partnership with Rangers to launch Spaceshot – a sort of spot-the-ball contest, which all concerned believed would be a sure-fire money-spinner. Spaceshot in fact proved too complicated for the United and

Rangers fans to grasp and lasted just two months. Most gleeful at this were Rangers' bitter rivals, Celtic. After all, Man United were supposed to be the Catholic club and have links with them.

United's own brand of lager – Red Devil – launched in 1987, wasn't too much of a success either. The club had generously offered one free ticket to Old Trafford for every fan who collected the required number of ring pulls: 640, to be exact. The scheme – introduced at a time when alcohol was being blamed for just about every problem in football – collapsed without Man United, so far as is known, giving away a single free ticket.

Despite a hefty salary and a prominent position in English football, Edwards borrowed heavily from the bank and owed them a considerable amount of money. In 1989 a chance presented itself to clear those debts in one fell swoop – it came in the shape of Michael Knighton. In return for a promise of an £80,000 a year salary and the post of chief executive for at least three years, Edwards gave Knighton the option to buy United for some £10 million. As the deal became public knowledge and it emerged that Knighton wasn't quite as wealthy as he'd first suggested, Edwards was humiliated. Not only had he appeared desperate to sell Manchester United but to

many it also looked as if he'd seriously undervalued the club.

In December 1989, Edwards tried to rectify this mistake when he entered negotiations with United director Amer Midani over the team's future ownership. These discussions broke down when Edwards demanded £15 million for his beloved Manchester United – an increase of 50 per cent in just three months. Midani was understandably a little miffed that he – a loyal member of the Man United board – was expected to fork out £5 million more than a ball-juggling outsider.

THE ONES THAT GOT AWAY

PETER SHILTON

Chose Forest over United, which saved him an extra 15-year wait for a Championship medal.

MARK LAWRENSON

Fergie wanted him around 1987 but he preferred to retire through injury.

MIGUEL ANGEL NADAL

The hunt for Nadal went on longer than the one for Lord Lucan and was similarly successful.

TERRY BUTCHER

Luckily for him, he broke his leg and had to stay at Rangers.

STUART PEARCE

Preferred to stay playing under Cloughie the autocrat rather than Fergie the dictator.

JUNINHO

Wanted to go to Spain, where matches are shown on Brazilian TV.

PAUL GASCOIGNE

United were unwilling to meet his terms, so he went to Spurs instead.

JOHN BARNES

United would have bought him from Watford, but scouting report was inconclusive.

DIEGO MARADONA

For some reason found Naples more suited to his lifestyle than Manchester.

GARY LINEKER

Barcelona offered him to United for £2.5 million in 1988 but the club 'couldn't afford it'.

ALAN SHEARER

First preferred Blackburn, then preferred Newcastle, now would prefer anywhere but ...

This is a team that could well have turned out wearing the colours of Manchester United, if things had turned out differently. They are all players who were on the verge of signing for United but somehow escaped that terrible fate.

Sub GLENN HODDLE

God must have told him he'd win more honours if he stayed at Tottenham.

Joint managers JOCK STEIN

Realised who still made the big decisions after one conversation with Matt Busby.

BRIAN CLOUGH

Chairman wanted him but Matt Busby apparently said, 'over my dead body'.

Manchester United	0	4	Nottingham Forest

54,375   Greenhoff B (og), Woodcock 2, Robertson

1977-78 season – 17 December 1977

Brian Clough's Nottingham Forest – promoted in 3rd place the season before – were, almost unbelievably, on top of the table. United were struggling in 14th spot. This was the match when the natural order would be restored: Forest would be found out and begin their descent to mid-table obscurity, while United would punish these Johnny-come-lately fly-by-nights and rise to a more seemly position as befitted their station. Instead, they got stuffed. Forest went on to win the Championship and it was United who finished in mid-table obscurity.

Man Utd: Roche, Nicholl, Houston, McIlroy, B. Greenhoff, Buchan, Coppell, J. Greenhoff, Pearson (Grimes), Macari, Hill

Nottingham Forest: Shilton, Anderson, Barrett, McGovern, Needham, Burns, O'Neill, Gemmill, Withe, Woodcock, Robertson

UNITED MAULED AS FOREST PUT ON THE STYLE

United boss, David Sexton said 'They showed us up. Much as it hurts to admit it, they could have doubled the score.'
***Daily Mirror*, 18 December 1977**

JIMMY HILL'S MATCH OF THE DAY VERDICT

I have not see a First Division defence so torn to pieces at home for many years. United goalkeeper Paddy Roche must have wondered what was happening. Forest could have had seven for John Robertson (twice) and Martin O'Neill missed easy chances.
John McGovern and Gemmill were brilliant in midfield, with O'Neill and Robertson electrifying on the wings.
United need a shake-up. They lack aggression up front and their defence is full of holes.
***News of the World*, 18 December 1977**

Videoton	1	0	Manchester United

Wittman   **25,000**

(1–1 on aggregate after extra time, Videoton win 5–4 on penalties)

UEFA Cup quarter-final 2nd leg, 20 March 1985

In the UEFA Cup quarter-finals, which contained such illustrious names as Real Madrid and Inter Milan, United had the seeming good fortune to draw unglamorous Videoton, from the even less glamorous town of Szekesfehervar in Hungary. United's players had only won the 1st leg 1–0, but still expected to stroll it against what appeared to be the poorest side left in the competition.

After scoring an early goal to level the tie, Videoton then played to their strengths, by setting out their stall for a penalty shootout. United were all over the Hungarians, had a blatant spot-kick turned down, missed a hatful of chances and were desperately unlucky to go out after the lottery of a penalty shootout. Tee hee.

Videoton: P. Disztl, Borsanzyi, L. Disztl, Horvath, Vegh, Burcsa, Vaszil (Gomori), Wittman, Palkovics, Szabo, Vadasz
Man Utd: Bailey, Gidman, McGrath, Hogg, Albiston, Strachan, Duxbury, Whiteside, Robson (Olsen), Stapleton, Hughes

VIDEO NASTY HITS UNITED

Penalty failures by Frank Stapleton and Mark Hughes in a dramatic shoot-out last night cost Manchester United a semi-final UEFA Cup place.

But it was horrific that the tie went to penalties at all because United should have won comfortably.

Hungarians Videoton mounted only one serious attack in the entire 120 minutes.

The frenzy of the shoot-out quickened when Stapleton shot high over the bar, only to be reprieved when Videoton's substitute Otto Gomori also missed the target.

Then Hughes saw his tame shot saved by goalkeeper Peter Disztl. This time there was no reprieve.

For Videoton and their 25,000 fans it was an Hungarian rhapsody as Imre Vadasz, scorer of the vital goal was deluged by excited, weeping team-mates. Dejected United manager Ron Atkinson said: " It's a bitterly disappointing way to end a quarter final we dominated from start to finish. In two and a half hours football, the only time they were in our penalty area was for the shoot out."

Daily Express, **21 March 1985**

"I'm sure I
overheard
someone
say there was a
bald-headed
coot around here
somewhere."

Arthur Albiston
gets the wrong
idea about
becoming
one of the
Busby babes.

PIN MANCHESTER ON THE MAP

Time limit: 2 hours

At last! A game you can play with all your Manchester United-loving chums. Just give them a pin – anything sharp will do – and ask them to point to where they think Manchester is. It's easy! Unless you support United of course. Afterwards, show them a map with the real answer on or, alternatively, get them to ask a Manchester City fan.

Advanced edition:
For this you will require a blindfold*. Give your Manchester United pals a much better chance of getting it right by blindfolding them first and then asking them to point at Manchester.
*Blindfold not supplied.

Liverpool	2	1	Manchester United

(after extra time)

A Kennedy, Whelan   100,000   Whiteside

Milk Cup Final, 26 March 1983

Most football fans know that Manchester United went 26 years without winning the League title. What is forgotten is that it took them 32 years to get their hands on the League Cup. In 1983 they were just 15 minutes away from winning, when Alan Kennedy equalised. The way United treat the competition now, it will probably be another 32 years before they win it again.

    Ironically, on the same day, George Best was making one of his last-ever comebacks, for Bournemouth in the Third Division.

Liverpool: Grobbelaar, Neal, Kennedy, Lawrenson, Whelan, Hansen, Dalglish, Lee, Rush, Johnston (Fairclough), Souness

Mancheter United: Bailey, Duxbury, Albiston, Moses, Moran (Macari), McQueen, Wilkins, Muhren, Stapleton, Whiteside, Coppell

BULL'S BLOOD FOR PAISLEY

The friendly hop which Alan Kennedy's long-distance shot took on the slick surface of a heavy Wembley pitch earned Liverpool belated justice in this Milk Cup Final. It sent the match into a half hour of extra time in which United's crippled and rejigged side could only hold on like exhausted boxers in the faint hope of surviving into a replay.

    Liverpool manager Bob Paisley used the bullfighting analogy to explain it all: 'It was a case of taking them into extra time before killing them off. It was like a bullfighter before the last stab when the bull has about 40 arrows in its back.'

***Observer*, 27 March 1983**

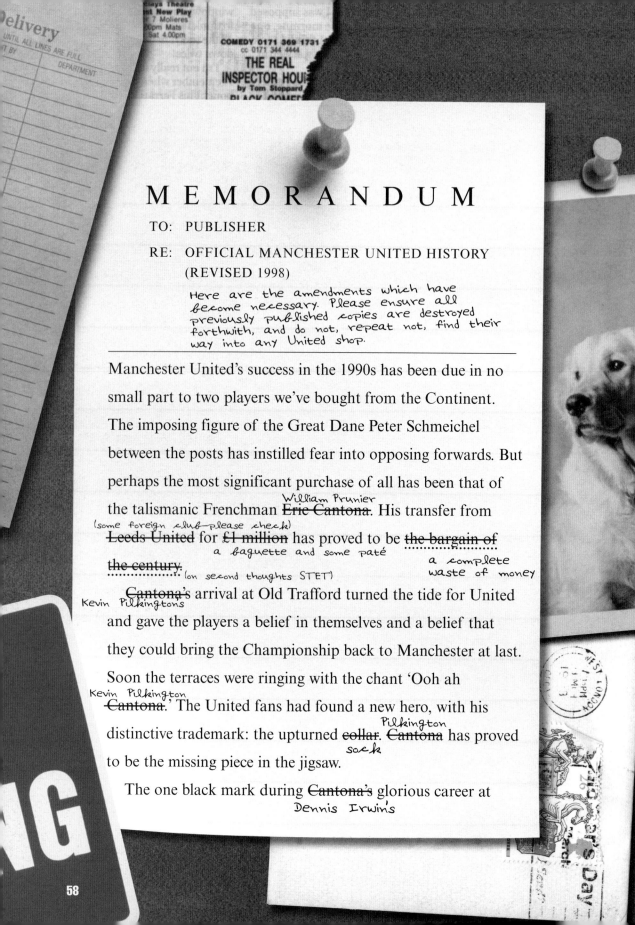

MEMORANDUM

TO: PUBLISHER

RE: OFFICIAL MANCHESTER UNITED HISTORY
(REVISED 1998)

Here are the amendments which have become necessary. Please ensure all previously published copies are destroyed forthwith, and do not, repeat not, find their way into any United shop.

Manchester United's success in the 1990s has been due in no small part to two players we've bought from the Continent. The imposing figure of the Great Dane Peter Schmeichel between the posts has instilled fear into opposing forwards. But perhaps the most significant purchase of all has been that of the talismanic Frenchman ~~Eric Cantona~~ *William Prunier*. His transfer from ~~Leeds United~~ *(some foreign club—please check)* for ~~£1 million~~ *a baguette and some paté* has proved to be ~~the bargain of the century.~~ *(on second thoughts STET)* *a complete waste of money*

~~Cantona~~'s *Kevin Pilkingtons* arrival at Old Trafford turned the tide for United and gave the players a belief in themselves and a belief that they could bring the Championship back to Manchester at last. Soon the terraces were ringing with the chant 'Ooh ah ~~Cantona~~ *Kevin Pilkington*.' The United fans had found a new hero, with his distinctive trademark: the upturned ~~collar~~ *Pilkington*. ~~Cantona~~ *sock* has proved to be the missing piece in the jigsaw.

The one black mark during ~~Cantona's~~ *Dennis Irwin's* glorious career at

United so far was the unfortunate occasion ~~at Selhurst Park,~~ ~~when he became involved in a fracas with a member of the~~ ~~crowd, in the so-called 'kung fu incident'. Cantona lashed out~~ ~~under great provocation from a spectator, who it later transpired~~ ~~was himself no angel.~~

the cost of two nights rental

The player immediately regretted his actions and apologized to the club. He was fined and suspended by

Blockbusters till the following October.

~~Manchester United for the rest of the season.~~ (After the court case, he willingly took football training with groups of

(cut this out of date nonsense)

underprivileged youngsters as part of his community service.)

Being a ~~Frenchman, Eric Cantona~~ is nothing less than an

an Englishman, Andy Cole

artist, a thinker, a philosopher, a poet and that rarest of creatures a footballing intellectual. His profound observations on leaving

the pitch

~~court~~ became the most quoted words of the year: '~~When the~~

I'm just here to do a job, y'know. Obviously, y'know,

~~seagulls follow the trawler, it is because they think sardines will~~

I'm glad to score goals, but it don't matter at the end of the day

~~be thrown into the sea.'~~ *who scores em, as long as the team win.*

(As long as Eric Cantona remains at Old Trafford, continued success is virtually assured. Eric has told manager Alex Ferguson that he wishes to end his career at Manchester United, so he should be here for many many years to come. One thing we can be certain of, though, is that Eric Cantona's name will never ever be forgotten.) ◄— *might need to lose all this*

EXCUSES 2

Q.
Why was the London-born Scottish singer Rod Stewart blamed for Manchester United losing the 1991–2 Championship?

A.
Because he held a concert at Old Trafford. Manchester United plc decided, in summer 1991, that the long-needed repairs to their threadbare pitch should be postponed in order to stage a Rod Stewart gig. At least, this was the threadbare excuse given by their fans as soon as the team lost three of their last four matches and Leeds took the title.

Q
What reason, apart from a Rod Stewart concert of course, was given by United fans for their team being thrashed 4–1 on New Years' Day by Queens Park Rangers?

A
The players had overdone their celebrations of Alex Ferguson's 50th birthday the previous day. These rumours were strenuously denied by the club, who put down United's abysmal showing to a flu outbreak. Good to know that it was nothing to do with Man United playing rubbish. On 1 January 1996, the players were no doubt suffering the after-effects of honouring Ferguson reaching the grand old age of 54 when they were pummelled 4–1 by Tottenham. And on New Year's Day 1974, they were unaccountably celebrating the Ayr United No. 9's 32nd birthday when they went down 3–0, again to QPR.

EXCUSES

Q.
What reason did Manchester United give for not buying Juninho from Middlesbrough in summer 1997?

A.
He was too small. According to Manchester United's chief executive Martin Edwards, the club did not require a diminutive, pint-sized, 5 foot 5 inch, Brazilian wizard. 'We have a lot of smallish players and, if you bring Juninho in, it's another small one in our squad.' What Edwards didn't want to admit is that Juninho didn't want to go to Old Trafford in the first place, bizarrely preferring Atlético Madrid.

Q. What reason did Alex Ferguson give for Manchester United going 3–0 down at half-time at Southampton in 1996?

A. They were wearing grey shirts. 'The players could hardly pick one another out.' If the grey shirts made the United players invisible, wouldn't that have given the Southampton defenders a problem? The players trotted out for the second half in blue and white, and the grey shirts were discarded for ever, having never been worn during a United victory. Days later the disgraced shirts had been reduced in the United shop from £36.99 to £14.99. There were few takers – but then again the fans probably couldn't see them.

Stuart Pearson
and Martin Buchan
model the John Steed
avengers look, while
back in the changing
rooms Tommy Docherty
struggles to get into his
Emma Peel outfit.

Ron Atkinson
explains how
he threw away
a ten-point
lead –
Just like that.

Joe Jordan modelling the short-lived away kit for the pre-season tour of the Highlands.

DEAR M

ENCLOSED IS AN IDEA FOR
NEXT SEASON'S ENSEMBLE,
WHICH IS BRILLIANT
IN MY OPINION.
IT WOULD TIE IN
WITH PLANS TO
REDESIGN OLD TRAFFORD
LIKE A GIGANTIC SHIP.
THE SHIRTS MUST BE
LIGHTWEIGHT COTTON, THE
SHORTS VERY TIGHT TO
SHOW OFF THE LOVELY
TIGHT BUTTOCKS. I'VE
ALSO DESIGNED A
FETCHING RUBBER NUMBER
FOR AWAY GAMES.
YOURS

JEAN-PAUL

Dear M,

Just a few ideas as promised on the new Manchester United strip — trust this was what you had in mind. Decided against including a quiver full of arrows into the design — we don't want the boys to look foolish, after all. Green for the shirts, I think. Red is very yesterday. There is a hunting cap, which completes the outfit but could cause problems when going up for headers.

Regards
Vivienne

CHAMPIONSHIP FLOPS

NUMBER THREE

1985-1986

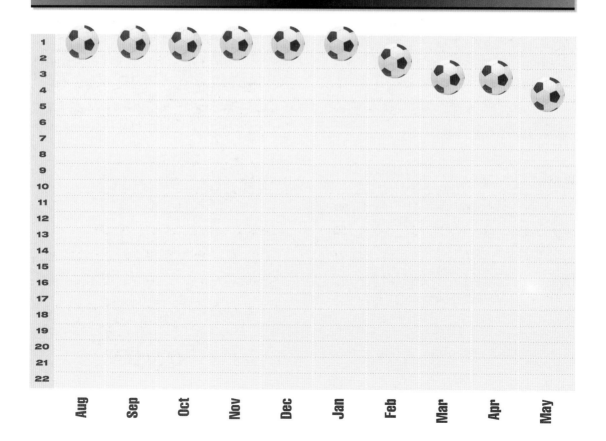

With the millstone of 19 seasons since they last won the League title hanging round their necks, 1985–6 was surely going to be the campaign when that great burden was finally lifted. At the start of the season, everything that could go wrong did go wrong, as United won their first ten matches. By Bonfire Night, they were unbeaten after 15 games, and ten points clear of the rest. In short, disaster beckoned. The title was theirs for the taking, it was in the bag, the rest of the League might as well just pack up and go home.

Then on 9 November, Bryan Robson limped off against Sheffield Wednesday. They lost the match, their unbeaten record and their illusion of infallibility. Home draws with Spurs and Watford and a 3–0 mauling by mighty Leicester City immediately followed.

It's not easy to squander a ten-point lead. It takes ineptitude, buffoonery and sheer haplessness. And by February, United had finally achieved it, losing the lead they had held since the opening day to Aston Villa. They never regained it or showed any signs of regaining it, as defeats in March by Southampton and QPR showed.

United's slumps in form coincided with Bryan Robson's injuries: hamstring in November, ligaments in February, dislocated shoulder in March. In fact, during this time Robson was rumoured to have made more appearances on *A Question Of Sport* than he did for United – although during one episode, he did limp off injured after 23 minutes during the mystery guest round.

The fight had gone out of United, their confidence had long since evaporated and their football had turned as flat as Big Ron's two-day-old champagne. Meanwhile, the title race was fought out in their absence by Liverpool and Everton. On the last day of the campaign, United even managed to lose third place – to West Ham. A season that had begun with ten straight wins turned out to be their worst for five years.

Before and after the Sheffield Wednesday match:

	P	W	D	L	F	A	Pts
Before	15	13	2	0	35	6	41
After	27	9	8	10	35	30	35

28.9.85

	P	W	D	L	F	A	Pts
Man United	10	10	0	0	27	3	30
Liverpool	10	6	3	1	25	11	21
Chelsea	10	5	3	2	14	10	18

Final Table

	P	W	D	L	F	A	Pts
Liverpool	42	26	10	6	86	37	88
Everton	42	26	8	8	87	41	86
West Ham	42	26	6	10	74	40	84
Man United	42	22	10	10	70	36	76

WHERE THE FANS SIT AT
OLD TRAFFORD

A. The Norfolk Contingent

B. The Suffolk Contingent

C. The St Neots Branch, Man Utd. Supporters' Club

D. The 'Which one's Eric Cantona' section

E. Junior Reds (with direct tunnel access to Club Shop)

F. The 'We've had to remortgage the house to come here, but we don't mind' section

G. Celebrity fans' area

H. Minor celebrity fans' area (restricted view)

I. Mick Hucknall's entourage

J. Referees' Association (United Supporters' Branch)

K. The Hardline 'I wish we'd never won the bloody title now' section

L. Friends of Martin Edwards

M. Players' wives/girlfriends

N. Girls allegedly linked with Ryan Giggs

O. Poached Youth Players' section

P. Greater Manchester Undertakers' Association (motto: it's all about getting bodies in the box)

Q. The 'Disappear once Man United start losing' section (sometimes empty by 4.05)

R. The 'It were all better in Johnny Carey's day' section

S. Daytrippers

T. Sunday drivers, yeah

U. The 'You could hear a pin drop in this section' section

V. Mancunians

W. Dug out – Ferguson, Kidd and McClair sit here

X. The 'Had no interest in football before it became fashionable' section

Y. Away fans

Z. Pitch

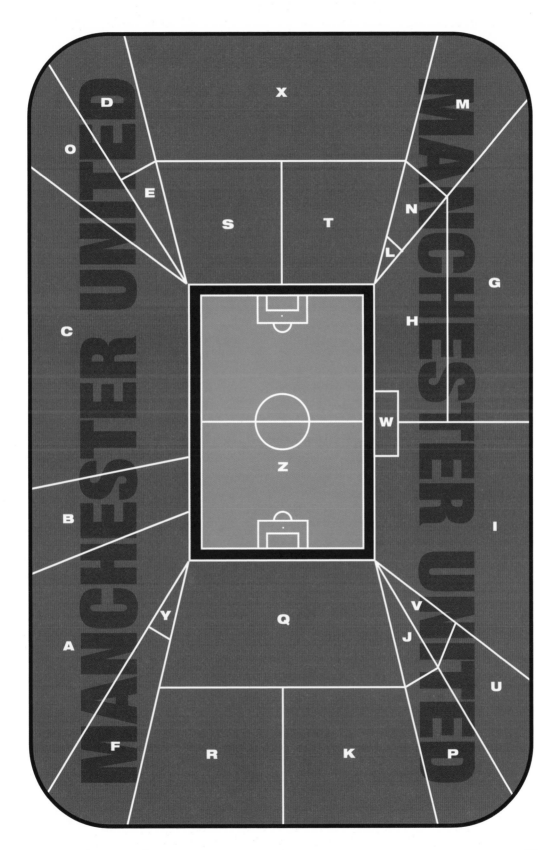

HOW MUCH DO YOU HATE MAN UNITED?

1 Your team will win the League if Manchester United beat your nearest rivals. Do you:
(a) Start chanting, 'Come on you Reds' at the top of your voice?
(b) Count your blessings, you'll be happy either way?
(c) Pray for United to lose – after all, there's always next year?

2 United get a penalty in the eighth minute of injury. Do you:
(a) Say, 'Oh well, there have been one or two injuries'?
(b) Tut?
(c) Apply to the European Court of Human Rights to have the result overturned?

3 Your mum is taken ill on the same day that United lose. Are you:
(a) Miserable?
(b) Filled with mixed feelings?
(c) Ecstatic?

4 Your six year old decides he wants to support United. Do you:
(a) Understand that it's his decision?
(b) Stop his pocket money?
(c) Leave him on a motorway hard shoulder 300 miles from home?

5 A former United first teamer is transferred to your club. Do you:
(a) Think, 'Oh well, he plays for us now'?
(b) Be over-critical of any mistake he makes?
(c) Start supporting your local crown green bowling team instead?

6 England reach the World Cup Final with a team containing 11 United players. Do you:
(a) Support the lads – it's England after all?
(b) Watch the team but try to stay neutral?
(c) Seek asylum in Iraq and apply for citizenship, claiming cultural oppression?

7 United are live on telly and getting thrashed 4–0. Your partner chooses this moment to say he or she will leave you unless you turn off the TV and talk things over. Do you:
(a) Switch off the set and talk? Your relationship is much more important than one football match.
(b) Think, 'Oh well, I'm taping it anyway for my collection'!
(c) Have a two-word conversation without taking your eyes off the set and fail to notice the banging of the front door?

8 A misguided aunt buys you a United shirt. Do you:
(a) Wear it? It feels comfortable and besides it's what a lot of people are wearing these days.
(b) Wear it only when your aunt comes round otherwise she'll be upset?
(c) Stage a rooftop demonstration at your aunt's house, during which you ritually burn the shirt?

9 Your boyfriend only gets turned on if you shout out the names of Manchester United players. Do you:
(a) Comply? After all, he is your boyfriend.
(b) Seriously consider ending the relationship?
(c) Shout out the names, 'Ralph Milne, Paddy Roche, Mike Phelan …' and watch what happens?

10 A distant uncle dies, leaving you a substantial number of shares in Manchester United plc. Do you:
(a) Decide United aren't so bad after all?
(b) Immediately sell the shares and enjoy a luxury cruise in the Caribbean?
(c) Keep the shares, use your huge influence in the money markets to buy a majority shareholding, take over as Chairman, then do nothing, allowing the club to stagnate for years and years?

If mostly (a):
You're clearly a Manchester United supporter and don't even know it. You'd almost think you had red blood pouring through your veins. Get back to Basingstoke or wherever it is you come from. Go on, clear off!

If mostly (b):
Oh dear! Come on, get off that fence, you'll get blisters, you lily-livered, wishy-washy, namby-pamby, closet-United-loving so-and-so.

If mostly (c):
That's more like it. Keep up the good work. If there were more people like you, the world would be a nicer, friendlier place.

Birmingham City	5	1	Manchester United

Dillon, Buckley 2, 23,550 Jordan
Givens, Calderwood

1978–9 season – 11 November 1978

This was one of those scorelines that the bloke who reads out the football reports has to read twice. Most people would have sat bolt upright on hearing this result, shocked not only by the margin of victory but also by the realisation that Birmingham City were in the same division as Manchester United. Birmingham's outstanding player was Argentinian World Cup winner Alberto Tarantini, whose massive perm belied his hard-man image. He tormented the United defenders with his brilliance. In a bizarre accident in the same match Brian Greenhoff was knocked unconscious. Greenhoff's only consolation was that during this time he was United's best player. This was one of just six League matches that Birmingham won all season, and they were relegated, having given us a good laugh along the way.

Birmingham C: Freeman, Tarantini, Dennis, Towers, Gallagher, Page, Dillon, Buckley, Givens, Calderwood, Fox
Man Utd: Roche, Nicholl (Albiston), Houston, McCreery, B. Greenhoff, Buchan, Coppell, J. Greenhoff, Jordan, Macari, McIlroy

STOP ALBERTO!

Birmingham manager Jim Smith lashed out last night against the threat of a growing campaign to ruin Alberto Tarantini's career in English football.

The Argentinian left England defender Brian Greenhoff unconscious for 26 minutes on Saturday when he also clashed with Joe Jordan and Manchester United's assistant manager Tommy Cavanagh.

But Smith saddened by these ugly stains on his struggling side's 5–1 victory claimed: 'Certain players tried to intimidate Alberto hoping he would react badly and get himself into trouble.

'My big fear now is that other teams will make a calculated effort to provoke Alberto.'

Daily Mirror, **13 November 1978**

BIG CITY FM

TONY SPENCER

It's 20 minutes to the top of the hour, here on Big City FM, the number one sound in London. So how was your weekend, you people out there in radioland? I had a stonking time, watching the old soccer match up in that great city we all know as Manchester. Flying up on the shuttle with a few of my mates from the biz, to lend the lads a bit of much-needed support. Although to tell you the truth, I'm not sure they could hear us behind that half-inch thick smoked glass.

Everyone was there. Er ... Angus, Chris, let's see, there was Zoe, Posh, Pete of course, and I think Dani was around somewhere. In fact, she was up and down most of the afternoon. But what a stonking match, people. United were all over the other team, um, the ones with the, er, white shirts and the black trim on the shorts. You know the ones I mean. Great game, great game. The best moment for me was halfway through the second bit, when Mick turned up out of the blue. He had planned to get here for the kick-off, but had a bit of bother parking. I've had the same problem with my helicopter, I don't mind telling you.

United scored three great goals. I remember them all so clearly. During the first one I was chatting to Zoe, the second I was having a drink with Angus and Chris, and when the third one went in, we were still watching the slow-motion replay from the second! Late on in the game, the other side scored a couple of goals themselves. In the end it was a relief to hear the final whistle – for me, an hour and a half is just a little too long to be watching soccer. It's what I call too much of a good thing. And I know some of the fans think the same as me, 'cos plenty of them were leaving ten minutes from the end. So come on you football authorities – shorter games. It's what the fans out there are crying out for.

Well
people, we had set up a bit of a meet with one or two
of the better-known players in the United bar afterwards, although the
post-match interviews did cause a bit of a delay. But, er, we didn't keep Ryan
and David waiting for too long. I asked Ryan why I hadn't seen him pulling on
the old England shirt, and he told me that he is in fact Welsh. I wonder
how many of you people out there knew that.

So,
as I was telling Teddy, I can't wait for next Saturday,
when I'll be going to see the mighty Reds play Tottenham Hotspur –
that's at, er, White Hart Lane. I haven't been there since, ooh, it must have
been about '93. What a stonking sport that American Football was
for a very short time.

But
all this has got me into thinking – and
not for the first time, people – seeing as how Man U
have so many of us fans down here in the smoke, something
should be done. I mean, you only had to look around the shuttle at all
the red shirts, red scarves and one or two of the old red noses. So Tony
Spencer's Big Monday Idea this week is – wouldn't it be sensible for
Manchester United to relocate to London? It would certainly make it a heck of a
lot easier for the dyed-in-the-wool fans, like Angus, Zoe, Chris and myself, to fit a
game into our busy schedules.

So come on Man United – how about moving to London? It's what the
fans are crying out for.

Now here's Jennifer with a travel update...

Torpedo Moscow | 0 | 0 | Manchester United

(0–0 on aggregate after extra time, Torpedo win 4–3 on penalties)

11,357

UEFA Cup 1st round 2nd leg, 29 September 1992

This was a tie that took some losing. Three and a half hours without conceding (or scoring) a goal, going 2–0 up in the penalty shootout, and United still managed to blow it. Unlike the Videoton tie, some seven years earlier, it was Manchester United who were under the cosh this time. They were happy to settle for the post-match penalties, having not yet learnt that they were rubbish at them. At least this time Mark Hughes was saved from the ignominy of missing a vital spot-kick – by getting himself sent off.

Torpedo Moscow: Podshivalov, Sillimonov, Cheltsov, Asanasiev, Vostrosablin (Savichev, Shustikov, Grishin, Talalayev, Arafiev (Ulyanov), Chuganov

Manchester United: Schmeichel, Irwin, Phelan (Parker), Bruce, Webb, Pallister, Wallace (Robson), Ince, McClair, Hughes, Giggs

TORPEDO SHOOT DOWN UNITED

SODDEN DEATH

Manager Alex Ferguson pledged an inquest into Manchester United's goal famine after their bizarre exit from the UEFA Cup on a rain-swept evening in Moscow.

United contrived to lose the penalty shoot-out against Torpedo after going two-up.

Steve Bruce, Brian McClair and then centre-half Gary Pallister all missed from the spot with a second round place in their pockets.

Torpedo triumphed 4–3 as the traumatic contest reached a sudden-death stage.

Ferguson admitted: 'It is deeply disappointing to lose a shoot-out after going two ahead.

'We should have finished them off before that. We were the better side at Old Trafford and the better side tonight.

'But we didn't score and we're out.'

Ironically Ferguson decided against practicing penalties in training this week and never even discussed who might be the principal takers.

It was a policy that rebounded with a vengeance after last night's second goalless stalemate.

And Ferguson added: 'When it reached the penalty showdown. I really didn't fancy us.'

Graham Fisher,
Today, 30 September 1992

DRUBBINGS – 6

Ipswich Town	6	0	Manchester United

Mariner 3, Brazil 2, Thijssen   30,120

1979–80 season – 1 March 1980

1 March 1980: the Saturday when all our dreams came true. You might think that the scoreline is astonishing enough – it is; read it again and enjoy once more that feeling of astonishment. But the score masks a even more amazing story. Ipswich Town were awarded two penalties and managed to miss both – and they still won 6-0. Let's just write that again: 6–0.

    This was no bumping-along-the-foot-of-the-table United, either. At the time of the match and at the end of the season, they were second. In fact, they lost the title by the two points they surrendered so easily at Portman Road.

'UNITED ARE LUCKY THEY DIDN'T GET HUMILIATED BY A SIXTEEN GOAL BEATING'

Daily Mirror, 3 March 1988

Ipswich: Cooper, Burley, Beattie, Thijssen, Osborne, Butcher, Mills, Muhren, Mariner, Brazil, Gates
Man Utd: Bailey, Nicholl (Jovanovic), Houston, McIlroy, McQueen, Buchan, Coppell, Sloan, Jordan, Macari, Grimes

A result for Ipswich to savour and United to shudder about. United have not been so humiliated for a long time.
    They performed as if freshly graduated from a crash course in buffoonery, littering the game with ghastly mistakes and conceding two needless penalties both of which were saved. This marvellous win brought Ipswich a club record of 15 games without defeat and even if they had been in form Manchester would have struggled to contain such attractive opposition as Mariner plundered a hat-trick and Brazil narrowly missed one.
Observer, **2 March 1980**

JIMMY RIMMER

Played 34 games in nine years for United, before going on to win the Championship and European Cup with Aston Villa.

PAUL McGRATH

Ferguson thought he was finished but he still had another eight years left in the top flight.

KEVIN MORAN

Went to try his luck in Spain with Sporting Gijon, before contributing to Blackburn's dramatic rise.

DEINIOL GRAHAM

Played just one league game for United before going on to bigger and better things with Emley.

ANDREI KANCHELSKIS

Long-running feud with Ferguson ended with transfer to Everton.

GORDON STRACHAN

Sold by Ferguson at both Aberdeen and Man United, went on to spur Leeds United to the Championship at United's expense.

DAVID PLATT

Got rid of for nominal fee to mighty Crewe at the age of 19 without ever playing for the first team.

KEITH GILLESPIE

Makeweight in Andy Cole deal to Newcastle, which estimated his worth as one-seventh of Cole's.

PETER BEARDSLEY

Bought from and sold back to Vancouver Whitecaps after his United career had lasted 45 minutes of a Cup tie against Bournemouth.

MARK ROBINS

His goals took Man United to the 1990 Cup Final, but Ferguson declared that he 'was not a United player'. He soon wasn't.

DION DUBLIN

Sold on to Coventry after just 12 games and one broken leg, long before his England potential was ever spotted.

These players were all let go by Manchester United long before their careers had reached their peaks, in many cases for little or no money.

Sub **ANDY RICHIE**

A goal every other game for United was rewarded by a transfer to Brighton in 1980, after which he scored over 160 goals for his four clubs.

Manager **DAVE SEXTON**

Sacked after winning last seven matches of 1980–81 season.

Oxford United	2	1	Manchester United

Lawrence, Biggins   13,912   Graham

Milk Cup 4th round 2nd replay, 19 December 1983

Oxford United	2	0	Manchester United

Saunders, Briggs   12,658

Littlewoods Cup quarter-final, 20 January 1988

In the mid-1980s, Oxford United were the League Cup specialists, whoever the sponsors happened to be that year. In 1983, they were a Third Division side on the way up; in 1988, they were a First Division team on their way down – but it hardly mattered as long as they were playing Man United in a Cup match. By the time of the second game, Oxford had achieved something Manchester United had failed to achieve since 1960 – they'd had their name engraved on the trophy.

1983
Oxford: Hardwick, Hinshelwood, McDonald, Thomas, Briggs, Shotton, Lawrence, Whatmore (Biggins), Vinter, Hebberd, Brock
Man Utd: Wealands, Moses, Albiston, Wilkins, Moran, Duxbury, Robson (Macari), Muhren, Stapleton, Whiteside, Graham

1988
Oxford: Judge, Bardsley, Dreyer, Shelton, Briggs, Caton, Hebberd, Foyle (Whitehurst), Saunders, Phillips, Rhoades-Brown
Man Utd: Turner, Anderson, C. Gibson, Blackmore, Moran (Hogg), Duxbury, Robson, Strachan (Davenport), McClair, Whiteside, Olsen

OXFORD TERRIERS SHATTER UNITED

And Smith Did Score

BY LAURA TAYLOR

SOME DATES change history. In football, Saturday 21 May 1983 is one such occasion. As every schoolboy knows, this was the date when Brighton & Hove Albion first won the FA Cup. Little did we realise then what a turning point this would be. Three more FA Cups and five Championship crowns have since followed. These days, on almost every street in every town, you'll see kids decked out in replica Brighton kits – a sight unthinkable 15 years ago. The amazing rise of Brighton has been mirrored by the sensational descent of their victims on that May afternoon, Manchester United. Looking back, it's hard to believe that it was Brighton who were the overwhelming underdogs.

This week, I met up with the man who made it all possible, with his glorious winner in the final minute of extra time. Who could forget commentator Brian Moore's excited words, 'And Smith must score – and does!'. Sir Gordon Smith, who bagged two goals on that fateful day, will certainly never forget. 'I remember it like it was yesterday,' reflects Brighton's Life President, the still trim Sir Gordon, 43, speaking in his palatial Sussex home. 'I drew the keeper and slotted it home to make it 3–2. Within seconds, the game was over. The first person to congratulate me was Steve Foster, who as everyone knows had missed the Final through suspension. Still, we more than made up for it on Fossie's behalf in 1984, when we did the Double. I mean, with players like Moseley, Gatting,

Howlett, Smillie and Grealish in your side, how could you go wrong?'

On the other hand, things most definitely did go wrong for Manchester United. While the star-studded Brighton & Hove Albion team was strolling to the title, United found themselves adrift at the foot of the table, virtually doomed to relegation by Christmas. Still, with players like Robson, Wilkins, Stapleton and

Whiteside, they were always going to struggle in the top flight. I wondered if Sir Gordon felt any sympathy for United's plight. 'Of course, it's always sad to see a once great club rooted to the bottom of Division Three. When they just survived against Hereford last season, I was relieved that they won, in a way. After all, it was my goal that began their decline.'

Sir Gordon believes the appointment of Graeme Souness as the new manager may help turn the corner for United, but there have been many other false dawns at this now-comatose giant. One remembers the

short-lived tenures of Alan Ball, Graham Taylor, Dr Josef Venglos, Alex Ferguson, Steve Coppell (for one week), Bryan Robson and others too awful to mention, who all arrived full of promise and soon departed, having delivered nothing. The final ignominy for United's few remaining supporters was the sale of their ground, Old Trafford – ironically to developers who built a Seagulls Superstore on the site. Manchester United now find themselves homeless and bankrupt, with Altrincham and Rochdale the latest clubs to turn down requests to ground-share.

There is only one cloud on Brighton's horizon. It still rankles with Sir Gordon that, despite being the biggest club side in the world these days, the town in which the team is least popular is Brighton itself. The colours that predominate on the seafront are the green and white of Bognor Regis Town. The only people not to resent the fortnightly intrusion of tens of thousands of recent converts are Brighton's hoteliers. 'I'm sick and tired of hearing local people talk the club down,' said the Scots-born magnate. 'If I had a pound for every time I'd overheard someone say to an Albion fan, "What part of Brighton are you from?" I'd be a millionaire.'

Sir Gordon and Lady Smith now spend much of the year travelling the world as goodwill ambassadors for the club. 'It's amazing. For some foreigners, the only English they know is "Brighton & Hove Albion" or "Tony Grealish". I was in Nepal with Jimmy (now Lord) Melia last year, and one Sherpa came over and proudly showed us his Seagulls tattoo.'

As Brighton & Hove Albion continue to expand abroad – with Superstores now in 158 countries – it's on their doorstep that the club face perhaps their biggest fight. The club's plans to demolish Brighton Pavilion and replace it with an 80,000 capacity stadium are still going full steam ahead, despite vociferous local opposition. Sir Gordon scoffs at the heritage lobby's attempts to save the palace. 'It's just an old building,' says Sir Gordon. 'And let's face it, Brighton & Hove Albion these days are a lot bigger than the town.'

Everton	5	0	Manchester United

Sheedy 2, Heath, Stevens, Sharp   40,769

1984–5 season – 27 October 1984

Watford	5	1	Manchester United

Callaghan 2, West, Blissett, Jackett   20,047   Moran

1984–5 season – 13 May 1985

The morning papers billed Everton at home to Manchester United as a battle of equals between the two main pretenders to Liverpool's crown. It was nothing of the sort. United's championship challenge turned out to be about as short-lived as Big Ron's suntan, and faded even faster.

It was one thing to lose to the champions and quite another to go down 5–1 to a team that had only escaped relegation the week before.

On the morning of their last match of the league season, United were in the runners-up spot; they finished fourth. Perhaps they preferred it that way – this was the period when United had made fourth place their own.

Everton: Southall, Stevens, Mountfield, Ratcliffe, Van Den Houwe, Steven, Reid, Bracewell, Sheedy (Gray), Heath, Sharp
Manchester United: Bailey, Moran (Stapleton), McQueen, Hogg, Albiston, Strachan, Moses, Robson, Olsen, Hughes, Brazil

Watford: Coton, Sinnott, Rostron, Taylor, Terry, McClelland, Callaghan, Blissett, West, Jackett, Barnes.
Man Utd: Bailey, Gidman, Albiston, Whiteside, McGrath, Moran, Duxbury, Strachan, Hughes, Stapleton, Brazil

DISUNITED THEY FALL

Perhaps the Championship will stay in Merseyside after all. Everton stated their case thunderously yesterday, overwhelming Manchester United as thoroughly as the 5-0 scoreline suggests.

United were not so much beaten as destroyed, their credibility in tatters as their hugely expensive collection of talents came off second best in every area of the field, Everton's greater appetite and determination winning every battle.

The Observer, **28 October 1984**

UNITED CRASH

BLUE MURDER AT GOODISON

MANAGER
TOMMY DOCHERTY

1972–7

If Frank O'Farrell was chalk, then his replacement Tommy Docherty was certainly cheese. Although he had an undistinguished career in club management, never staying anywhere too long, the Doc could talk an excellent match. Before becoming Manchester United manager, Tommy Docherty's career had been going in a downward spiral: from FC Porto to assistant manager of Hull City to Scotland manager. His career finally bottomed out at Manchester United.

Whatever else the Doc achieved before or after his time at Old Trafford, we should always be grateful to him for one thing: he got Manchester United relegated. Despite Frank O'Farrell having laid the groundwork, in his first season Docherty failed to get them relegated by just seven points. However, in 1973–74, he made no mistake. It hadn't taken him long to put his distinctive stamp on a bad team – by making them worse.

Whereas his predecessor had been criticised for his reluctance to buy new players, Docherty brandished the chequebook like it was someone else's money. His expensive purchases – Alex Forsyth, George Graham, Jim McCalliog and Jim Holton – may have been good enough to play for Scotland, but the First Division was another matter entirely. Docherty had the answer to that, and soon they were playing in the Second Division.

Perhaps Tommy Docherty's greatest skill as a manager was that of falling out with his players. United hero Denis Law's ten years at Old Trafford were ended unceremoniously by a free transfer to the local enemy Manchester City. The Doc's actions backfired on him when Law scored the goal that sent United down. According to Docherty, some of the old stars were less interested in how well they played for United than how long they played.

It was perhaps typical of Docherty that his highpoint as Manchester United manager should be immediately followed by his lowest point, when he was dismissed six weeks after winning the 1977 FA Cup. The previous season, he had made United a laughing stock by losing the Cup Final to 2nd Division Southampton. But he outdid himself again by starting an affair with Mary Brown, the wife of United's physiotherapist Laurie Brown.

The liaison had been going on in secret for two years when the Doc decided, on the night of the Cup Final win against Liverpool, that now was exactly the right time to tell the United directors that he was an adulterer. And more to the point, that the cuckold in this case was their physio Laurie Brown. The tabloids had their field day, as expected, but just when the story was beginning to die, Louis Edwards issued a denial that Docherty would be sacked. Sure enough, when the Doc turned up for work the next day, he discovered the electricity in his office had been disconnected.

The United board were unable to tell him to his face that he was losing his job over the affair with Mrs Brown. Instead, according to Docherty, chairman's son Martin Edwards accused him of selling Cup Final tickets. He refused their request for him to resign, so they sacked him. He said afterwards, 'I've been punished for falling in love. What I've done has got nothing to do with my track record as a manager'. It was true that they had ignored his track record, otherwise he'd surely have been sacked after taking them down to the Second Division.

'CLUB WIVES OUST DOC'

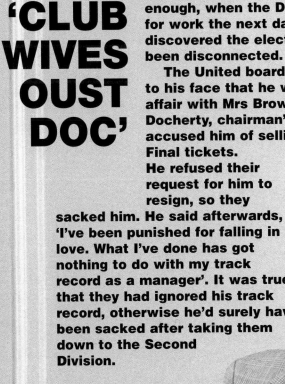

EXCUSES 4

Q.

In 1997–8, how was a car park responsible for Manchester United being knocked out of the European Cup and losing their way in the Premiership?

A.

Because they were forced to play on a pitch built on top of a car park. United were delighted when the European Cup quarter-final draw pitted them against Monaco, perceived to be the softest touch left in the competition. After the 0–0 draw in the away leg, Alex Ferguson complained that eight of his players had calf injuries. He attributed these to the hardness of the Monaco pitch, which he blamed on the fact that the turf had been laid directly over a car park. Three days later, United lost 2–0 at Sheffield Wednesday. Once again, according to Fergie, the pitch was at fault. 'It's a disappointment but perhaps predictable after the week we've had, and then to play on a heavy pitch like this. That's two bad pitches in a row. I don't think we can have any complaints.' Curiously, the United manager failed to blame the pitch for United's defeat by Arsenal the following week or their subsequent elimination from Europe by Monaco. Both matches were played at Old Trafford.

Q.

What was Bryan Robson's excuse for failing a breath test in 1988?

A.

He had attended some arduous business meetings. The United and England skipper was found by police on a slip road of the M62, standing next to his car, which had run out of petrol. After failing a breathalyzer test and refusing to give a urine sample, he was taken to court and subsequently banned for three years. In court, Robson's lawyer said he had been involved in a number of difficult business meetings, which apparently was not a euphemism along the lines of tired and emotional. Robson had perhaps had other arduous business six years earlier, when he was banned for a year for drink-driving.

Manchester City	5	1	Manchester United

Oldfield 2, Morley, Bishop, Hinchcliffe   43,246   **Hughes**

1989–90 season – 23 September 1989

Winston Churchill was Prime Minister the last time Man United suffered a worse derby defeat. The City faithful were euphoric as they made the short trip home, while the United fans – on what was for most of them one of the longest away trips of the season – made their excuses and left early. The manager's own excuses were doubtless drowned out by the cries of 'Ferguson out' coming from the few remaining United supporters.

Manchester City: Cooper, Fleming, Hinchcliffe, Bishop, Gayle, Redmond, White, Morley, Oldfield, Brightwell, Lake (Beckford)
Manchester United: Leighton, Anderson, Donaghy, Duxbury, Phelan, Pallister, Beardsmore,(Sharpe), Ince, McClair, Hughes, Wallace.

AGONY FOR SAD FERGIE - UNITED CRISIS

Manchester United, the country's most glamorous and best supported club, reduced their fans to tears on Saturday.

From boardroom to dressing-room United are showing all the classic signs of a club cracking up – and the man being singled out as the scapegoat is manager Alex Ferguson.

United's disgruntled supporters angrily chanted "Fergie out", while the rival fans taunted "what a waste of money!"

The £13 million investment in a team that Fergie built looks more like Jerry-built.

Daily Mirror, **25 Sept, 1989**

GUTLESS!

Tommy Docherty last night pointed an accusing finger at MANCHESTER UNITED'S humiliated, highly-paid superstars and claimed:

"Some of them just haven't got the heart or pride you expect from players wearing those red shirts – it's a disgrace."

The former United boss watched in disbelief as Manchester City tore his old team to shreds with effortless ease in a 5-1 rout.

And it left the outspoken Scot putting the blame fairly and squarely at the feet of the expensively assembled players.

He said: "That's the worst they have played since Crystal Palace hammered them 5-0 the week before I took over ... and that's going back as far as 1972."

"It all goes to show that you just can't buy success or loyalty. Some of those players out there just weren't fit to pull on a United shirt."

The Doc is spot on. Despite a staggering investment of £13m, United boss Alex Ferguson still hasn't got it right.

Daily Star, **25 Sept 1989**

FLEDGLING FERGIE

IT WAS EARLY 1954, AND IN THE FERGUSON HOUSEHOLD ALEX AND HIS BROTHER WERE PLAYING SNAKES AND LADDERS...

FUME!

TEE HEE! THAT'S YOU DOWN ANOTHER SNAKE, ALEX!

SIX! HOORAY, I'VE WON THE GAME! BAD LUCK ALEX!

GRR! THAT DICE WAS TOO HEAVY, WE WERE PLAYING ON THE WRONG KIND OF BOARD, THE WIND WAS BLOWING IN THE WRONG DIRECTION...

THAT'S IT FOR TONIGHT LADS. OFF TO BED NOW.

OCH, DAD! SURELY YOU'RE GOING TO ALLOW ME SOME EXTRA TIME SO I CAN WIN. IT'S NOT FAIR OTHERWISE.

CALM DOWN ALEX, IT'S ONLY A GAME.

HOW CAN YOU SAY THAT? THAT WAS THE WORST BIT OF ADJUDICATION IN ALL MY SEVEN YEARS OF PLAYING SNAKES AND LADDERS. COULD YOU NOT SEE HE WAS RAISING HIS GAME TO OBSCENE LEVELS?

OFF TO BED WI' YOU — YOU'VE AN IMPORTANT SCHOOL MATCH TOMORROW!

NEXT DAY AT SCHOOL...

SO CHILDREN, THIS IS HOW THE POOR SCOTTISH FORCES OF BONNIE PRINCE CHARLIE WERE THRASHED BY THE SASSENACHS. THERE WAS VERY LITTLE THEY COULD DO.

MILLIONS OF EVIL SASSENACHS

A FEW GALLANT SCOTS

WITH ALL DUE RESPECT MISS McTAVISH, YOU'RE TALKING ABSOLUTE RUBBISH.

OH YES, ALEXANDER?

OUR TROOPS WERE WEARING THE WRONG KIND OF ARMOUR. THEY SHOULD HAVE CHANGED COLOURS AT HALF TIME.

THE PRINCE'S TACTICS WERE HIGHLY QUESTIONABLE ON THE DAY. IF HE'D PLAYED A FLAT BACK 4000 AND ALLOWED THE ATTACKERS TO GET IN FROM THE WINGS BEHIND THEIR DEFENCE WE'D HAVE SLAUGHTERED THEM.

GOAL!!

HEROIC SCOTS

DING! DING!

ALL RIGHT CHILDREN, OFF YOU GO!

NO, I HAVEN'T FINISHED, AND ACCORDING TO MY WATCH THERE'S AT LEAST EIGHT MINUTES LEFT. YOU'VE FORGOTTEN TO ADD ON THE TIME IT TOOK WEE TOMMY BREWSTER TO TAKE A MESSAGE TO THE HEADMASTER.

FIVE MINUTES LATER...

AND REMEMBER THE BELL IS A SIGNAL FOR ME, NOT FOR YOU. AND FURTHERMORE... HANG ABOUT, WHERE'S EVERYBODY GONE? BAH!

Manchester United	3	3	Galatasaray

Robson, Hakan (og), Cantona 39,396 **Arif, Turkyilmaz 2**

European Cup 2nd round 1st leg, 20 October 1993

Galatasaray	0	0	Manchester United

40,000

European Cup 2nd round 2nd leg, 3 November 1993

After 15 minutes of the home tie against Galatasaray, everything was going according to plan, God was in heaven and all was right with the world. United were 2–0 up and coasting to a place in the Champions League proper. The inevitable tabloid predictions about turkeys being stuffed seemed to be coming true. An hour later, Man United were 3–2 down and their proud 37-year unbeaten home record in Europe was in jeopardy.

Cantona's late equaliser meant all United had to do now was go to Istanbul and win. Those tabloid comments had deeply offended the Turks and United's reception was appropriately hostile. The team did nothing to endear themselves to their hosts, by constantly bleating to the referee about time-wasting. Eric Cantona got himself sent off after the final whistle by expressing himself freely to the Swiss referee in his native tongue, perhaps not realising that the official was a French teacher. Sacre bleu!

CANTONA IS SENT OFF TO COMPLETE UNITED MISERY

English football suffered its second crushing blow in four weeks last night when Manchester United were knocked out of the European Cup by Galatasary of Turkey. This setback follows the defeat in Holland that virtually ended England's hopes of appearing in the finals of the 1994 World Cup.

And, as if that were not bad enough, United's Eric Cantona was sent off here in an undignified scene after the final whistle.

The temperamental French international was shown the red card by Swiss referee Kurt Rothlisberger for something the player said to him. Cantona had complained throughout about Galatasaray's time-wasting tactics, and he went straight up to the match official at the end of the game.

After shaking Rothlisberger, a teacher of French, by the hand, the Frenchman pointed to his own eyes and obviously expressed an opinion of the referee's handling of the problem that was not at all flattering. It had Rothlisberger reaching angrily for the red card and flourishing it over the Frenchman as he punched the ball away in frustration. It had not been a happy night for Cantona.

His tall, strong German marker, Reinhard Stumpf, did not give him an inch of room and, in doing so, put a question mark against the decision of United manager Alex Ferguson to leave out Mark Hughes.

***Telegraph*, 4 Nov 1993**

1st leg
Man Utd: Schmeichel, Martin, Sharpe, Bruce, Keane, Pallister, Robson (Phelan), Ince, Cantona, Hughes, Giggs
Galatasaray: Hayrettin, Stumpf, Bulent, Ugur, Gotz, Tugay, Arif, Hamza, Hakan, Suat (Yusuf), Turkyilmaz (Erdal)

2nd leg
Galatasaray: Hayrettin, Yusuf, Gotz, Stumpf, Hamza, Arif (Ugor), Suat, Tugay, Bulent, Turkyilmaz, Hakan
Man United: Schmeichel, Phelan (G. Neville), Bruce, Parker, Irwin, Keane (Dublin), Robson, Ince, Giggs, Cantona, Sharpe

EXCUSES 5

Q.
Why did Manchester United have so many players sent off in the mid-1990s?

A.
Because they wore a black away strip. According to a leading sports psychologist, 'It creates bad influences within the squad and will usually end in violence.' This was said days after black-shirted Eric Cantona jumped two-footed into the Crystal Palace crowd and of course totally accounts for his actions. If only this had been offered up as a mitigating circumstance before the Croydon Magistrates Court, the case would surely have been summarily dismissed.

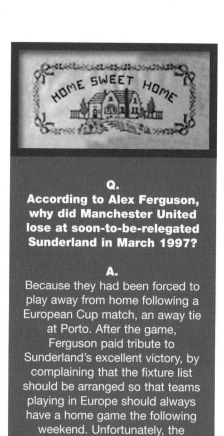

Q.
According to Alex Ferguson, why did Manchester United lose at soon-to-be-relegated Sunderland in March 1997?

A.
Because they had been forced to play away from home following a European Cup match, an away tie at Porto. After the game, Ferguson paid tribute to Sunderland's excellent victory, by complaining that the fixture list should be arranged so that teams playing in Europe should always have a home game the following weekend. Unfortunately, the League fixtures had already been decided the previous year, and Premiership officials would no doubt have assumed, on previous form, that United would be long out of Europe by this time.

AFC Bournemouth	2	0	Manchester United

Graham, Thompson   **15,000**

FA Cup 3rd round, 7 January 1984

Three weeks after losing to Oxford in the Milk Cup, United went out of the FA Cup to an even lowlier Third Division team. In losing to Bournemouth, who at that time were in the relegation zone, Manchester United made perhaps the most embarrassing defence of the FA Cup in living memory. In fact, they allowed Bournemouth to go beyond the 3rd round for the first time in 24 years.

Former Dean Court stalwart George Best, summarising on the radio, said 'If I were one of the United players, I'd be too embarrassed to pick up my wages.' Perhaps even more astonishing than the defeat was that Best had turned up and was allegedly sober.

Bournemouth: Leigh, La Ronde, Sulley, Savage, Brown, Brignoll, Train, Nightingale, Morgan, M. Graham, Thompson.
Manchester United: Bailey, Moses, Albiston (Macari), Wilkins, Duxbury, Hogg, Robson, Muhren, Stapleton, Whiteside, A. Graham.

NOW ATKINSON MUST PUT THE QUESTION

RON ATKINSON faces his disgraced players this morning needing to find an answer to an unpalatable question.

For the MANCHESTER UNITED boss can no longer avoid asking: "Why won't you fight for me?"

Maybe he should consult Bournemouth manager Harry Redknapp, for the former West Ham winger, like his Third Division colleague at Oxford, Jim Smith, knew all about United's worrying soft centre.

His team were a credit to his organisational talent and his ability to instil the right attitude.

Bournemouth's non-stop hustle made nonsense of United's reputation and when Milton Graham snapped up a dreadful miss by Gary Bailey it was time for the celebrations to begin. That was in the 62nd minute and two minutes later the little stadium literally shook in acclamation of a second, decisive goal from Ian Thompson.

Daily Star, 9 Jan 1984

DISGRACED

HARRY REDKNAPP'S Bournemouth Cinderellas, a collection of castoffs and misfits, sent Manchester United creeping away from Bournemouth last night full of shame and remorse.

Bournemouth struggling near the bottom of the Third Division, added to the FA Cup's romantic history by flattening the holders so comprehensively that United manager Ron Atkinson kept them locked inside their dressing room for 45 minutes.

You could detect raised voices from the corridor and when the players finally emerged, some famous faces were white and drawn.

Atkinson, normally so voluble, came briskly to the point: "All I am prepared to say is that this performance was a disgrace to the name of this club."

News of the World, 8 Jan, 1984

CHAMPIONSHIP FLOPS

NUMBER FOUR

1991-1992

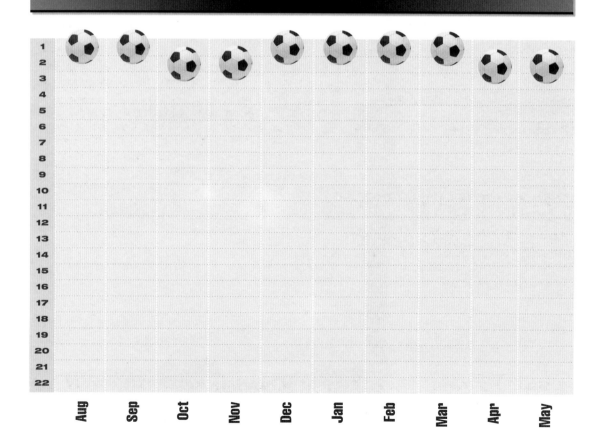

With the millstone of a quarter of a century since last they won the League title hanging round their necks, the 1991–2 season was surely going to be the campaign when that great burden was finally lifted. By New Year's Day, United were top of the League and had lost only once all season. However, on the United horizon were two clouds without silver linings: that unbeaten record – as in 1985–6 – had been lost at Sheffield Wednesday; and, more importantly, they had failed to shake off the challenge of Leeds United.

On that glorious first day of 1992, QPR slaughtered United 4–1 at Old Trafford and Leeds were in front once again. The two Uniteds took it in turns at the top until Easter, when Manchester appeared to have finally got their noses in front in what had long been a two-horse race. Two points clear with a game in hand, and entering the final furlong – the final furlong in this case being their four remaining matches. A week later, Man United had doubled their defeats for the season and the Championship had gone to Leeds.

'I thought the West Ham performance was obscene in the sense of the effort they put into the match ... It was almost criminal to see all that effort.'

ALEX FERGUSON

IT'S TORTURE FOR FERGIE

Foul-up No. 1: 20 April – Ferguson chose this moment to drop Mark Hughes for the home game with Nottingham Forest and play with one recognised striker – that is, if you can bring yourself to recognise Brian McClair as a striker. United went down to a shock 2–1 defeat while Leeds beat Coventry.

Foul-up No. 2: – 22 April – United only had to turn up at Upton Park to take the points off soon-to-be-relegated West Ham. They didn't take any. A hopeful cross from the right, a hapless clearance by Pallister, and the world's longest bobble off a shin from 20 yards by Kenny Brown, gave the Hammers the only goal of the game. Things got so desperate, Alex Ferguson even chucked on his own son as a substitute.

The United manager, in a manner which he has since trademarked, accused West Ham of raising their game to what he called 'obscene levels' – completely ignoring the fact that the Londoners were fighting to avoid the drop. United's game in hand had now disappeared.

Foul-up No. 3: 26 April – Leeds had that morning won their penultimate fixture away at Sheffield United, with an excellent own goal by Brian Gayle. They were now four points clear, having played a game more. United had to win at Anfield and hope that Leeds lost their final match. This day became Manchester United's ultimate nightmare: not only did they lose the title but they also lost it at Anfield, going down 2–0. Within one short week, they had thrown away nine months of hard work. At the final whistle, one of two things happened: either the Kop applauded United's gallant efforts so close; or they chanted, 'You lost the League on Merseyside.' You decide.

Leeds United's millstone of having gone 18 years without winning the Championship was finally lifted.

18.4.92

	P	W	D	L	F	A	Pts
Man United	38	20	15	3	59	27	75
Leeds United	39	19	16	4	68	35	73

2.5.92 Final Table

	P	W	D	L	F	A	Pts
Leeds United	42	22	16	4	74	37	82
Man United	42	21	15	7	63	33	78

R.I.P.

UNCLE DEREK

✠

DIE HARD MANCUNIAN

WHO NEVER MISSED AN AWAY RESERVE MATCH,
AND WHO DIED TRAGICALLY, FOLLOWING A CHILL
CAUGHT ON THE TERRACES WATCHING HIS BELOVED
UNITED GRIND OUT A TEDIOUS GOALLESS DRAW
WITH OLDHAM RESERVES

11.30 a.m. Saturday morning. Anfield. Sitting in the half-empty Kemlyn Road stand, the north wind whipping into my face, bringing with it freezing cold sleet. Ten minutes to go and the game's still goalless. There hasn't been a shot on target since the pre-match kickabout. Life really doesn't get much better than this. Magic!

I tell you, this is real football. This is what being a proper fan's all about. Going to watch the reserves stick one up the Mersey scum. All right, so I should have gone to me Uncle Derek's funeral, but I'm sure it's what he would have wanted. Hang on – there's action on the far touchline. Brian McClair's warming up. We must be settling for the nil–nil.

Things started going wrong as far as I'm concerned, when we won the title in '93. Before that, you could at least expect to hear one or two local accents spoken in the Stretford End. And you could get to your seat without falling over bags full of tat from the United shop. 'Are we playing in red this week?' you'd hear them ask. 'When we watch this on telly, will we be behind the goal on the left or the right?' Bloody daytrippers. In the end I just stopped going. Like any true fan.

I watch the reserves instead. You can see the players of the future before they start earning a million a year, and before they've even shagged a single pop star.

I'm proud to say that I know some of these players better than I know my own kids. Certainly better than Alex Ferguson does. When did we last see him at a reserve match? Like today, for example. For some reason, he seems to think it's more important to prepare for the home match against Blackburn.

These part-time fans – they can't remember anything about a game until they go home and watch the replays from 14 different angles. Time was, if you were looking the other way when a goal went in, that was it. You'd missed it. Tough luck. Although it never stopped you having an opinion about it in the pub after. Now every Tom, Dirk and Olaf think they have a right to sound off.

Oh aye, McClair's sat down again. Eighty-five minutes gone. If this was a first-team game, most of the bloody part-timers would be in the car on their way home by now. Me, I'd rather leave a match in a pine box than head off before the final whistle.

Wait a minute – what's he doing? The ref's only gone and abandoned the game. Brilliant – I can come back and watch the rematch Tuesday morning. Besides, this gives me more time to set off to the big one – the B team's crunch match against Morecambe Reserves.

Stand Up If You Hate Newton Heath

Part Two

Ernest Dobbins stood outside Newton Heath's ground, which was mysteriously empty. The cab driver had left only a minute before, so Ernest was easily able to catch up with him, by walking briskly.

'You! Cabbie!' exclaimed Ernest. 'What's happened to the association football match? You know something, don't you, you rum cove?'

'Oh, didn't you know sir?' sneered the cabbie. 'You being a supporter who wears t'favours of Newton Heath, surely you must have heard – they moved last week.'

'Then why did you bring me here?' 'I'm a cabbie, sir. We're trained to take t'long route.' 'So where is the game taking place then, you blackguard?' 'Well sir, Newton Heath want to become t'biggest football club in t'world. So to that end, they've moved to Clayton.' 'Well take me there now!' entreated Ernest. 'And don't spare the horse.'

Ernest took his place in the crowd just as the Newton Heath and Burnley players were taking the field. There were gasps from the crowd as they realised the home side were no longer wearing their traditional yellow and green shirts, but were instead clothed in red vestments and white knickerbockers.

'What's happened to tradition?' cried a gentleman behind Ernest. 'Why, it's only a decade since they last changed their apparel.'

'Hear hear!' agreed Ernest. 'I really do object to lining the players' pockets. Why, I hear one of the players is nothing more than a laudanum fiend and regularly wears an open collar in the presence of ladies!'

Sadly for Ernest, his words were lost in his beard and no one heard him. He turned his attention to the Newton Heath team, as they lined up for the kick-off.

'No place for young McClair yet again,' he announced to no one in particular. 'Even though Cassidy has been suspended for bringing the game into disrepute for not having a moustache. And I see Fitzsimmons is playing, despite being only 50–50 in the week after losing his left leg to gangrene. And I declare that floppy-haired outside-right's play has actually improved since he commenced stepping out with posh music hall – or Lily Langtry as some call her.'

Yet again, Ernest's words were lost, this time over the terrible sound of the man beside him coughing up blood into his kerchief. Typical, thought Ernest. I always end up standing next to the bloke with tuberculosis. By this time, the crowd was starting to get restless. Two minutes gone and still no goals. Then Newton Heath scored the opener. Charlton, a player always recognisable by his distinctive comb-over moustache, rifled home a long-range sizzler from all of 4 yards. The crowd went as wild as the manners of the times deemed acceptable.

'Hurrah,' said Ernest. 'Hurrah,' agreed Ernest's companion, in a break between coughing fits.

'Sir, do I detect from your "Hurrah" that you do not hail from these parts.'

'Indeed, sir,' he spluttered. 'I have come here for today's game from the Antipodes.'

'By Jove, that must be a singularly arduous journey,' said Ernest.

'On the contrary – it has taken me but

three years. Having reached this Holy Grail, I shall now be the envy of every inhabitant of Wagga Wagga. Everyone there supports Newton Heath, or at least they did when I left in 1890.'

'Yes, in the last few years these bandwagon supporters have sprung up from nowhere,' declared Ernest. 'None of them knows anything of the history of this club before 1878.'

'There was no club before 1878. That was the year they were founded as Newton Heath Lancashire and Yorkshire Railways,' he wheezed.

'Yes, of course, I remember the chant, "Give us an N".'

Ernest and his new-found companion were so engrossed in their perorations, they realised they hadn't been paying attention to the match and had missed five goals. At that moment, they saw young Keane hack down the Burnley winger and the referee unaccountably indicate a foul. Keane found cause to debate the decision and was cautioned, for talking back to the official before they had been formally introduced. The Burnley winger was soon on

his feet, though, helped by the trainer who had ministered the magic opium.

Ernest and his new companion were to remain lifelong friends, since the Australian passed away soon after half-time, leaving Ernest with no one to talk to.

Oh well, he hasn't missed much, Ernest thought, as Newton Heath bundled in an equaliser for the seventh time that afternoon. Eight-all, he thought, as we move into injury time.

Over on the far touchline, he could see the agitated figure of the Newton Heath secretary-manager, an excitable Scotchman, reminding the referee of how many minutes were left to play, by vehemently tapping on the face of the grandfather clock he always took to matches. After 15 minutes, the Heathens scored the winner and the official blew his whistle to end the match.

Stepping over the prone body of his dead friend, Ernest made his way to the Newton Heath Emporium, where he procured a splendid pair of replica knickerbockers. He wondered whether he should celebrate Newton Heath's triumph by heading for a nearby den of iniquity, where the lowest of all humanity would gather in sordid squalor and moral degradation, and he would most certainly catch syphilis and die an agonising death in penury.

Well, maybe just a swift one, he thought, and headed off into the night.

Southampton	4	1	Manchester United

Lawrence, D. Wallace,   17,915   Davenport
Le Tissier 2

Littlewoods Cup 3rd round replay, 4 November 1986

Plucky United, fourth from bottom of the First Division, had done well to hold the Saints at Old Trafford, but with Southampton on home territory the gap in class soon told. For United players like Chris Turner, Graeme Hogg, Peter Davenport and Colin Gibson, this was their Cup Final.

Immediately after the match, United boss Ron Atkinson was given a vote of no-confidence by chairman Martin Edwards. 'I don't feel inclined to make a comment about the manager.' The problem for Big Ron was that there was more silverware around his neck than in the United trophy cabinet. Two days later he was sacked. Still, at least he now had a proper use for all that suntan lotion.

Southampton: Shilton, Forrest, Dennis, Case, Wright, Gittens, Lawrence, Cockerill, Clarke, Baker, Wallace, (Le Tissier).
Manchester United: Turner, Duxbury, Albiston, Whiteside (Wood), McGrath, Hogg, Moses, Olsen, Stapleton, Davenport, C. Gibson (Moran).

UNITED ARE POLISHED OFF BY A MATT FINISH

An unknown, who cost nothing, humiliated the multi-million pound miseries of Manchester United last night.

Matthew Le Tissier, an 18 year-old Channel Islander, celebrated his first ever goals for Southampton to provide the knockout to United's Littlewoods Cup demise: It was another sad and often depressing night for United boss Ron Atkinson, who must feel he has destroyed a litter of black cats – such are his distressing fortunes.

Already robbed of Bryan Robson and influential Gordon Strachan, among others, Atkinson must not have been able to believe how fate could be so cruel when both stand-in skipper Norman Whiteside and midfielder Colin Gibson both joined his out-of-action list before the interval.

Atkinson was obviously not as shell shocked as his side, for he said "I didn't think we were going to be beaten, the lads really battled." They worked tremendously hard to overcome the first half upsets, but unfortunately Jimmy Case ran the show in the second.
Daily Express, 5 Nov 1986

ForSale!ForSale!

**It walks. It talks.
It shouts its head off!**
Peter the goalkeeping doll. Pull his hamstring. Listen to him shout at his back four in a selection of European languages. Comes with glow-in-the-dark red nose.

United spectacles
Excellent for looking back at the 26 years between League titles. Allows the wearer to completely forget all those seasons of finishing 13th and the chants of 'Fergie out'. Lenses rose tinted only.

As spat out by Alex Ferguson!
Jaw-exercising taste sensation of the 1990s. Available in the following flavours: sour grapes; hard cheese; tough titties; sardine; invisible; spearmint.

Trophy polish
Spring clearance! We've got simply hundreds of unused, Euro-sized tins to give away.* Unexpected setback forces sale.

Relive those Champions' League triumphs!
Running time: till early March. Warning: may end sooner than expected.

George Best – The Complete Girlfriend Guide
After years of research, we're proud to present an up-to-date list of every blonde who's ever been linked with Belfast's favourite son.
Available soon: special Angie supplement.

The Martin Edwards mug
Eyes light up with pound signs. Look in his head – there's nothing there! Price subject to negotiation.

Still available!
The Brian McClair bench and pile cream set.

Order form
Yes, please rush me lots of overpriced United stuff. I understand that I am highly impressionable and that I live somewhere in the Home Counties. I also undertake to switch allegiance as soon as United start losing.
Name...
Address...
....
....
.... **Postcode**..................

* Well, not actually give.

UNITED for SALE

PART 2

THE MICHAEL KNIGHTON STORY

MARTIN EDWARDS, MAJORITY SHAREHOLDER OF MANCHESTER UNITED, WAS AT A LOOSE END...

IT'S MORE THAN 5 YEARS SINCE CAPTAIN BOB WAS THWARTED IN HIS ATTEMPT TO BUY MY CLUB. I'M ITCHING TO TRY AND SELL IT AGAIN.

MEANWHILE, IN A CASTLE IN AYRSHIRE...

I'M BORED! IT'S AT LEAST A YEAR SINCE I FAILED TO TAKE OVER BOLTON WANDERERS.

NOW WHAT CLUB SHALL I CLAIM TO BE A LIFELONG SUPPORTER OF THIS TIME?

WHY DON'T YOU LOOK IN YOUR I-SPY BOOK OF FOOTBALL TEAMS, DEAR?

I'VE GOT IT! **DARLINGTON!**

OR YOU COULD BUY MANCHESTER UNITED.

SOON, AT A SWANKY RESTAURANT...

I'M SORRY MR KNIGHTON BUT THERE'S NOTHING THAT WILL MAKE ME SELL MANCHESTER UNITED. IT'S MY LIFE! IT MEANS EVERYTHING TO ME!

I'LL GIVE YOU A LOT OF MONEY.

OH, ALL RIGHT THEN.

MEANWHILE, ALEX FERGUSON WAS PREPARING HIS TEAM FOR THE START OF A NEW SEASON...

WELL, WE SHOULD WALK THE CHAMPIONSHIP THIS SEASON, JUST AS LONG AS WE'RE NOT DISTRACTED BY A LONG DRAWN OUT AND ULTIMATELY UNSUCCESSFUL TAKEOVER BID.

OTHERWISE WE'LL PROBABLY FINISH ABOUT 13TH!

ALEX, I'VE BROUGHT SOMEONE TO MEET YOU.

MMM — HE SHOULD SLOT NICELY INTO MIDFIELD.

NO, HE'S YOUR NEW CHAIRMAN.

McGASP!

HELLO, I'M VERY RICH AND HAVE COME TO INVEST IN YOUR CLUB TO FURTHER ITS INTERESTS.

THE BANK MANAGER GOES ON...

THE THING IS, YOU SEE MR. KNIGHTON, THAT MOST OF YOUR WEALTH IS TIED UP IN PROPERTY AND OTHER HOLDINGS RATHER THAN READY CASH. FURTHERMORE YOUR ATTEMPT TO BRING IN BOB THORNTON OF DEBENHAMS FAME AND HIS PARTNER STANLEY COHEN HAS BACKFIRED SINCE A CONDITION OF THEIR INVOLVEMENT SEEMS TO BE THAT YOU TAKE A MINORITY INTEREST IN MANCHESTER UNITED FOOTBALL CLUB, AND YOU ARE NOW REGARDED BY EXPERTS AS A FIGURE WHO'S SOLE INTENT IS TO PURCHASE THE CLUB AND THEN SELL IT ON FOR A SUBSTANTIAL PROFIT. OH, AND WHILE I'VE BEEN SPEAKING, I'VE JUST HEARD THAT THORNTON AND COHEN HAVE DECIDED NOT TO GO AHEAD WITH THE DEAL. SO THAT LEAVES YOU BACK AT SQUARE ONE.

LUMME!

BORING BIT!

DRUBBINGS – 10

Liverpool	4	0	Manchester United

Beardsley 3, Barnes   35,726

1990–91 season – 16 September 1990

If Manchester City fans are obsessed by the desire to beat the team across Trafford Park, United supporters have a Liverpool fixation. So this 4–0 stuffing was all the more painful for them, especially as it was seen by millions of them live on terrestrial television.

Liverpool: Grobbelaar, Hysen, Burrows, Nicol, Whelan, Gillespie, Beardsley, Houghton, Rush, Barnes, McMahon
Manchester United: Sealey, Irwin, Blackmore, Bruce, Phelan, Pallister (Donaghy), Webb, Ince (Beardsmore), McClair, Robins, Hughes

BEARDSLEY PROVES WORST FEARS

The deepest fears of the First Division have been realised. Whispers of Liverpool's continuing superiority have been circulating around the country yesterday, in the first fixture of the season to be televised live, ominously ample confirmation was provided during their biggest defeat of Manchester United, their traditional rivals, for 65 years.

Beardsley, a United old boy who did not know that he had regained his place in Liverpool's line-up until an hour before kick-off, celebrated his comeback with three goals. The other was scored by Barnes, who can be comparatively reassured that he will stay in the side. All of them were gems.

They crowned a performance which progressed from uncharacteristic uneasiness at the start to a characteristic exhibition of their omnipotence by the end. Alex Ferguson, the United manager, who believes that he may be without Pallister for the European Cup Winners' Cup tie on Wednesday, had no doubts about Liverpool's quality.

"We didn't get any more than anyone else will here, I suppose," he said.
Stuart Jones, *The Times*, 17 September 1990

BOOZY UNITED

There had long been a tradition of boozing footballers at Old Trafford – one has only to think of George Best and Pat Crerand's nights on the town – but it was only during Ron Atkinson's tenure as manager that it seemed to affect the whole team.

In a short time, Big Ron collected together a group of players whose abilities were unrivalled when it came to getting tanked – both on and off the pitch. Ron Atkinson's laid-back approach meant that away from the training ground his players felt free to behave pretty well as they pleased. In some cases this meant drinking all afternoon. Regulars in the first team were also regulars in a string of pubs and clubs throughout Manchester. The players didn't feel they had any need to be discreet, as they weren't made to feel they were doing anything wrong.

From the time he made his debut as a 16-year-old, Norman Whiteside suffered inevitable comparison with his compatriot George Best. There was, though, only one way in which he could live with the master. Boozing. As time passed, Whiteside was still famous for his ability to weave this way and that – but, unfortunately for him, not on a football pitch. At least Norm wasn't alone. However much Whiteside could put away, there was Paul McGrath next to him putting away more. Despite its being common knowledge around Manchester, it took several years and a legendary bender in Malta in 1987 for their antics to hit the headlines.

The drinking habits of the United players were revealed by a shocked Arnold Muhren in his autobiography. He of course had emerged from a footballing education in which alcohol played little part and the whole culture was markedly different – East Anglia. He described United players coming into training still reeking from last night's beer. He couldn't understand the lack of attention paid to nutrition and a balanced diet – although it could be said his team-mates were consuming more than the recommended daily intake of wheat, barley, malt and hops.

As soon as Alex Ferguson joined the club in 1986, he knew exactly what to do about these drinkers – wait three years and then get rid of them. Whiteside was given a number of official warnings before being sold to Everton. McGrath was given an ultimatum to quit the booze or quit the game – he did neither, and joined Aston Villa. Robson was excused on the grounds that he didn't allow his drinking to affect his football, perhaps because he was usually injured.

MANAGER
DAVE SEXTON

1977–81

In 1972, United had appointed the flamboyant Tommy Docherty as a contrast to the aloof Frank O'Farrell. In 1977, after their experience with Docherty, they decided to opt for the aloof card again, by appointing Dave Sexton as manager. Shy, uncommunicative, uncomfortable talking to the press, with a successful record as a club manager – he was everything Tommy Docherty wasn't.

United weren't the first club to send for Sexton when they had tired of the Doc's ways – Chelsea had replaced the one with the other ten years before, and soon became a side that was not only fashionable but won trophies. Sexton was destined to fall short on both counts during his time at Old Trafford. There had been stories linking him with the United job dating back to 1971, but the United board obviously preferred O'Farrell's particular brand of aloofness. Sexton had to wait another six years for his chance, during which he'd taken Queens Park Rangers nearer to the League title than Man United had managed in the intervening time.

United had finally woken up and realised that they hadn't won the League Championship for ten years. For a club that regarded the title as their birthright, this failure was becoming a burden to United fans and a source of endless amusement to everyone else. Sexton's first season in charge ended, effectively, in January. After yet another hilarious New Year defeat, at home to Birmingham, which left them in 14th spot, they were knocked out of the FA Cup by West Brom. The rest of the campaign was a matter of fulfilling fixtures. In 1978–9, they improved on the previous season's tenth place, by finishing ninth.

Dave Sexton's greatest achievement as United manager was to assemble teams that could come within a hair's breadth of winning major trophies and then end up with nothing. We all treasure memories of the 1979 Cup Final, when United came back to equalise from two goals down with five minutes to go, only to concede the winning goal in injury time. The following season, Man United came as close to winning the League title as they had done since

1967. A 2–0 defeat away to Leeds United in their last match of the season handed the title to Liverpool by two points.

Dave Sexton had given himself a deadline of three years at Old Trafford in which to win a trophy, otherwise he'd go. Now those three years were up, Sexton decided to act decisively. He'd extend the deadline by another season – or by longer if United still hadn't won a trophy. Perhaps Sexton was hoping that his aloofness meant that no one had heard him make that promise in the first place.

Sexton had seen the difference the signing of Ray 'Butch' Wilkins had made to the side that finished runners-up, and was convinced that there was just one missing piece in the Old Trafford jigsaw for the 1980–81 season. That piece came in the unlikely shape of Garry Birtles – a man who soon made missing a speciality. Joe Jordan needed a consistent partner up front and he got him. You don't get more consistent than Birtles – no goals in 25 League matches.

United won the last seven matches of Sexton's final season in charge, during which time they rose from lowly 9th place all the way up to 8th. This wasn't enough to save him. He was fired five days after the end of the season for the very reason that he was hired in the first place – lack of flamboyance. Whatever players he put out on to the pitch, the team always seemed to reflect his character – they lacked flair, imagination and expression, and were rather dull, lifeless and grey. An average of 6,000 fans per match seemed to agree and stayed at home.

On the day Sexton was relieved of his job, he refused to give a single word of comment – which summed up more than any words his time in office.

SEXTON SACKED

Dave Sexton was sacked by Manchester United last night – to make way for Lawrie McMenemy.

Sexton was given the boot in a boardroom decision that ignored his recent success with seven straight wins. And that upset the United players.

England star Ray Wilkins was amazed by the decision which lined up Southampton manager McMenemy for one of the biggest jobs in football.

"I can hardly believe it," said Wilkins, "It must be some sort of world record for a manager to be sacked after seven wins in a row."

The United statement said: "It is the board's view that in spite of recent results, the team's performance has failed to live up to the high standard of football entertainment expected of Manchester United.

"This decision has been reached after taking into consideration the discontent amongst a predominant percentage of regular supporters."

PETER SCHMEICHEL

Ian Wright has crossed him off his Christmas card list.

REMI MOSES

Famous for crosses from the right, straight on to Jesper Olsen's face.

PAUL McGRATH

Frequently told complete strangers, 'You're my best pal.'

KEVIN MORAN

Did he ever finish a match without being stretchered off or sent off?

ROY KEANE

Did he ever finish a match?

PAUL INCE

Frequently called 'The Governor' but only by himself.

NOBBY STILES

Plenty of bite in the middle of the park – or should that be suck?

MICKEY THOMAS

The last person you'd want to borrow a fiver off.

NORMAN WHITESIDE

Enjoyed a drink, liked to foul, loved to mouth off – but at least he was good to his mother.

ERIC CANTONA

At home on any stage – Old Trafford, Wembley, Croydon Magistrates Court.

GEORGE BEST

Mainly a one-club man in his football career; a 1,857-club man in his private life.

Manager TOMMY DOCHERTY

If only there'd not been a bit on the side and more cups on the sideboard.

Sub BRYAN ROBSON

Famous for his 'good engine' – but drink driving bans meant it stayed in the garage.

| Manchester United | 2 | 2 | Southampton |

Kanchelskis, McClair   33,414   Gray, Shearer

Southampton won 4–2 on penalties (after extra time)

FA Cup 4th round replay, 5 February 1992

Having been 2–0 down, United only forced extra time and a penalty shootout when Brian McClair scored a fluky equaliser – wait for it – well into injury time. However, this extension just made the evening's finale all the more pleasurable.

Southampton earned a place in the 5th round and United earned a place in the record books – by becoming the first team from the First Division to be eliminated from the FA Cup on penalties.

Like penalty shootouts, Southampton have become United's nemesis. The 4–1 Littlewoods Cup thrashing had cost Ron Atkinson his job six years before. The glories of the 3–1 'grey shirts' debacle and the comical 6–3 tanking were still to come.

Manchester United: Schmeichel, Parker, Irwin, Donaghy (Sharpe), Webb, Pallister, Robson, Ince, McClair, Giggs, Kanchelskis (Hughes)
Southampton: Flowers, Kenna, Adams, Horne, Hall, Ruddock, Le Tissier, Cockerill, Shearer, Gray (Maddison), Benali

United manager Alex Ferguson was looking on the bright side: "In terms of games it will probably help our championship challenge."

UNITED GO OUT ON PENALTIES

Manchester United made the wrong kind of FA Cup history last night by becoming the first Division One club to go out of a competition steeped in tradition by the gimmicky method of penalty shoot-out.

England's Neil Webb and teenage Wales international Ryan Giggs will be the members of an expensive United line-up haunted by misses from the spot which allowed Southampton, strugglers at the opposite end of the First Division table, a surprise fifth round trip to Bolton.

Southampton did not even call upon their penalty expert Le Tissier and converted all four of the spot kicks they needed to take – each in front of a hostile Stretford End - to claim a victory which had looked assured in normal time when they took an early two-goal lead with Alex Ferguson's League and Cup favourites looking all at sea.

Daily Telegraph, **6 Feb 1992**

CHAMPIONSHIP FLOPS

NUMBER FIVE

1994-1995

At the start of the 1994–5 season, Manchester United had the millstone round their necks of having gone three months since last they won the League title. For the first three months of the season, it looked as though Newcastle United would be Man United's main rivals for the title, but that was before people realised Kevin Keegan's side were always champions in autumn and about 6th come spring. The real pretenders turned out to be Blackburn Rovers who, like the band of the same name, were famous for their brass in pocket.

Manchester United should have realised they weren't going to win the Premiership as early as 8 October. On the previous two occasions (1985–6 and 1991–2) that they had missed out on the title when it seemed easier to win it, they had tasted defeat at Sheffield Wednesday. This time was no different but for some reason United insisted on playing out the rest of the season.

Everything seemed to be going United's way when the two main contenders met at Ewood Park. A brilliant tackle by Blackburn's Henning Berg was rewarded with a red card and a penalty, which effectively turned the match – and, so it seemed at the time, the season – in United's favour.

However, the crucial turning points came in January. On the 10th, Alex Ferguson shocked the football world by buying Newcastle's Andy Cole for £7 million. Here was the missing piece in the jigsaw that would turn United from a Championship-winning side into Championship runners-up. Then on the 25th, Eric Cantona decided he'd like a little time off work and, to this end, *kung fu* kicked a Crystal Palace fan in the head.

Somehow, Manchester United clung on to the coat-tails of Blackburn, although by early April, Rovers had established an eight-point lead. It was at this time that Blackburn attempted to emulate United's form in the climax to the 1991–2 season. They lost matches at home to Manchester City and West Ham, so that by the last day of the season they were just two rather wobbly points ahead. The equation was simple: for Man United to snatch the title they had to win at West Ham while Blackburn drew or lost at Liverpool.

For Manchester United haters everywhere, this proved to be one of the longest hour and a halves since records began. For a time, all went swimmingly, as West Ham took a surprise lead while Blackburn went ahead at Anfield. Then came two equalisers which put the destination of the Premiership trophy in doubt. As the final whistles approached, a late goal for United would win them the title. Cometh the hour, cometh the man. Andy Cole won the title for Blackburn almost single-handedly, missing not only a host but also a hatful of chances. The late goal when it came was at Anfield, for Liverpool, but by then it was too late for United. When Jamie Redknapp's free kick went in, it was the Blackburn fans who started cheering as news came through that the final whistle had gone at Upton Park and Manchester United had blown it – their chances, not the whistle. The Liverpool fans were just as relieved as the Blackburn fans, as their team had been a whisker away from the awful irony of being responsible for United winning the Championship.

At least United supporters had the consolation of knowing that Andy Cole was indeed worth every penny of the £7 million – to Blackburn at any rate. They also had the consolation of the FA Cup Final six days later against unmighty Everton. There was no way Manchester United could finish runners-up in the two main domestic competitions. Was there?

Cole-apse!

Final Table

	P	W	D	L	F	A	Pts
Blackburn R	42	27	8	7	80	39	89
Man United	42	26	10	6	77	28	88

Manchester United	1	4	Queen's Park Rangers

McClair	38,554	Sinton, Bailey 3

1991–2 season – 1 January 1992

If only Manchester United could play all their matches on New Year's Day, they'd be in the Unibond League by now. United were top of the table, apparently heading for their first League title in 25 years. Step forward Dennis Bailey, a journeyman who came from nowhere and disappeared back there soon afterwards. But for at least 90 minutes of his life, we were grateful to him.

Manchester United: Schmeichel, Parker, Blackmore, Bruce, Webb, Pallister, Phelan (Giggs), Ince, McClair, Hughes, Sharpe
Queen's Park Rangers: Stejskal, Bardsley, Wilson, Wilkins, Peacock, McDonald, Holloway, Barker, Bailey, Wegerle, Sinton

BAILEY TREBLE HALTS SHABBY UNITED

Alex Ferguson, worried that Manchester United might lose concentration in between the three meetings with Leeds United, yesterday watched his worst fears realised.

A pitifully shabby impersonation of the side which had surged to the top of the First Division table, they left Old Trafford surrounded by the jeers they had earned during their heaviest defeat at home for 14 years.

There could be no excuses. The lone exception amid the listlessness and carelessness was Mark Hughes. Lively and alert, he gave the impression that he had avoided the excesses the night before. The rest did not.

Not Queen's Park Rangers though. Eager from the start, they took an early two-goal lead and might have added two or three more before becoming the first visitors to win at Old Trafford since Everton in March last year.

Ferguson made no attempt to disguise his side's deficiencies. "We never started," he said. "It was like a nightmare. We were totally outplayed. But I am sure that this will be a one-off."

Stuart Jones, *The Times*, 2 Jan 1992

OLSEN v MOSES

The incident that summed up the folly of Ron Atkinson's I'm-just-one-of-the-lads approach occurred in October 1986, during a routine training session. Perhaps the most shocking aspect of it was that it all resulted from a tackle by fey Danish winger Jesper Olsen, on United's self-styled hard man Remi Moses. According to Olsen, the following pithy exchange took place.

Moses: What the hell are you doing, you little idiot?

Olsen: What do you mean?

There swiftly followed a different kind of exchange, which led to Olsen being rushed to hospital with blood streaming from his left eye.

Eleven stitches later, the cover-up began. Big Ron, not for the first time, decided to turn a blind eye – as did Olsen, although as his was partially closed he didn't have much choice. Atkinson said, 'It's untrue there was any incident between the two players. It was a clash of heads ... a simple training accident. I was only four yards away from the action, I know what happened.' The trouble was, so did a group of journalists and photographers, who Atkinson had clearly forgotten were there too and who weren't inclined to back up Big Ron's rewriting of history.

The following month, two things happened: Ron Atkinson was shown the door by United; and Mike Tyson won the WBC heavyweight training accident championship.

FC Barcelona	4	0	Manchester United

Pallister (og), Romario,   114,000
Stoichkov, Ferrer

Champions League group A, 2 November 1994

This was to be the day when English football, as represented by Manchester United, would show that it was now the equal of Europe's best. In the event, Rotherham United might have been more worthy representatives, as Man United were trampled on by a vastly superior side.

Alex Ferguson had been doing his homework, and when it came to matchday his excuses were fully prepared and had never looked better. Shame about the team. UEFA's rule that clubs could only field five foreign players in European games was clearly to blame. Despite being fully aware of the ruling, Ferguson kept increasing his roster of non-English players, who were then unable to play together in Europe. In the Barcelona match, he dropped Peter Schmeichel in favour of Gary Walsh. It was a surprise that Ferguson didn't complain that Barcelona were able to play 11 foreigners – two Dutchmen, a Brazilian, a Bulgarian and seven Spaniards.

Barcelona: Busquets, Ferrer, Guardiola, Koeman, Abelardo, Bakero (Sanchez Jara), Amor, Stoichkov, Jordi (Ivan), Romario, Sergi.
Man Utd: Walsh, Parker, Bruce, Pallister, Irwin, Kanchelskis, Ince, Keane, Butt, Giggs (Scholes), Hughes

STANDARD-BEARERS TORN TO SHREDS

SLAUGHTERED, humiliated, chastened, Alex Ferguson was the one delving into the dictionary of dejection, laid low by Manchester United's drubbing in Barcelona, but he could have been speaking in general terms at the end of one of those weeks which serve to plant English feet back on the ground, if not, alas, on the ball.

It has been happening at fairly frequent intervals these past 40 years, since Hungary reinvented the game and scored six at Wembley, yet still there is genuine surprise when Johnny Foreigner proves the point all over again.

On Wednesday morning, The Paper That Supports Our Boys had trumpeted that English football was "ready to be acclaimed as the best in the world".

Twenty-four hours later, "our Premiership oaks" had been "cut down to size".

Saps might have been a better word, but the point this time was well made. It was, to use the adjective Ferguson finally settled for, a chastening week.

United were comprehensively outplayed, failing to muster a single shot on target, while Barcelona might easily have scored six. Nonplussed, Ferguson held up his hands and offered no excuses after the most emphatic defeat of his eight year management. Clearly he had been surprised by the quality of the Catalan side's play.
Joe Lovejoy, Sunday Times, 6 Nov 1994

I.F.K. Gothenburg	3	1	Manchester United

Blomqvist, Erlingmark,   36,350   Hughes
Kamark (pen.)

Champions League group A, 23 November 1994

Three weeks after the Barcelona debacle, United had a chance to make amends, against – in the obligatory phrase – a bunch of Swedish part-timers. The Gothenburg players, who had all returned to their normal jobs during Sweden's close-season, took time off work every other Wednesday to beat Europe's best in the Champions' Cup.

Manchester United desperately needed to win to keep alive any hopes of making the quarter-finals, and fully expected an easy victory, not least because over half of their opponents admitted to being United supporters. One of United's main tormentors was Stefan Rehn, a player considered not good enough for English football, after playing just four matches for Everton. As at Barcelona, Paul Ince showed that, when the going gets tough, the tough are often nowhere to be seen. The only time he was noticed was when he was sent off for dissent near the end.

IFK Gothenburg: Ravelli, Kamark, Johansson, Bjorklund, Nilsson, Martinsson (Wahlstedt), Erlingmark, Lindqvist, Blomqvist, Rehn, Pettersson (T. Andersson).
Man Utd: Walsh, May, (G Neville), Irwin, Bruce, Kanchelskis, Pallister, Cantona, Ince, McClair, Hughes, Davies (Butt).

UNITED RETURN IN SHAME AND SILENCE

The company of footballers returning from a humiliating night in Europe is not a recipe for Happy Hour. Aboard charter flight LEI 9586, the faces and the silence told the story of how far Manchester United fell short of expectations in Gothenburg on Wednesday.

They had flown to Sweden so sure of their ranking. Now they were separate beings. At the front, Sir Bobby Charlton, a director, sat Ramsey-like, his face white with shock. Behind him, Martin Edwards, the chairman, seemed in deep contemplation, wondering no doubt what to tell the shareholders at the annual meeting today after a 3-1 European Cup Champions' League defeat reckoned to have cost the club £7 million.

And Alex Ferguson, the United manager? Still reddened with anger and embarrassment, he looked unapproachable.
Rob Hughes, *The Times*, 25 Nov 1994

GOTHENBURG LEAVES HOPES HANGING

Foreign fields again proved hostile territory for Manchester United last night. Deserved defeat at Gothenburg's impregnable home means England's Double winners must overcome Galatasary on Dec 7, in the final round of Champions League Group A games, while praying the Swedes win at Barcelona. The future looks as bleak as the conditions at the Ullevi Stadium.

The Swede's technical and tactical superiority was apparent throughout this chilling encounter. To add insult to add insult to injury, Gothenburg's jubilant supporters stole the Stretford End's favourite chant:" Always look on the bright side of life."It was difficult.

Moments of brightness for United were as rare as sunlight yesterday. Paul Ince who failed to contain Gothenburg's playmaker, Stefan Rehn, was dismissed late on but, in reality, ignominy had already enveloped United.

Mark Hughes did manage to cancel out an effortless opener from the inspired Jester Blomqvist but within a minute Magnus Erlingmark had restored Gothenburg's advantage. Pontus Kamark's penalty simply helped condemn United to a fraught finale to the group.

EXCUSES 6

Q. Why did the Royal Mail drop Manchester United from their ad campaign?

A. They preferred Scunthorpe United. The Royal Mail prepared an advert for their 'I saw this and thought of you' campaign, featuring a Manchester United fan receiving a United badge through the post and jumping for joy. Market research then showed that Man United were so unpopular that the ad would alienate potential customers. The Royal Mail, possibly worried that people would find alternative methods to send their post, instead chose Scunthorpe. Their spokesman Steve Gaines said, 'We needed a team everyone could relate to.'

Q. According to the manager of the time, Tommy Docherty, who was to blame for Manchester United getting relegated in 1973–4?

A. United's coach driver. Docherty used the benefit of hindsight to suggest that it wasn't his or the players' fault but that of the bloke who drove the team to their away matches. 'I looked at everything possible that I could blame and the ultimate was really that the bus driver had to go. I mean, the cassettes he was playing in the bus were rubbish. He was late arriving to pick up the team. He was that late he drove so quickly that he got to the grounds too early … I think at the end of the day that he was to blame for us having such a bad season, or perhaps not.' Admittedly, his tongue was firmly in his cheek.

Manchester United	2	2	Rotor Volgograd

Scholes, Schmeichel   29,724   Nidergaus, Veretennikov

(2–2 on aggregate, Rotor win on away goals)

UEFA Cup 1st round 2nd leg, 26 September 1995

It was late September. The leaves were green and on the trees, the clocks were on British Summer Time, students were still at home poncing off their parents and Rangers hadn't yet tied up the Scottish League, when Manchester United were knocked out of Europe. The result was a pleasant surprise. Rotor Volgograd, their conquerors, were pretty much an unknown team, even in Russia. Yet a club that had still to win either their League or Cup came within seconds of achieving what no other team had managed in 39 years and 55 attempts – beating Manchester United at home. In the end, United had to depend on Peter Schmeichel to succeed where the outfield players had dismally failed – by heading home the equaliser.

This was the first tie ever won by Rotor Volgograd, in only their second ever European campaign.

Manchester United: Schmeichel, O'Kane (Scholes), P. Neville, Bruce, Sharpe, Pallister, Beckham, (Cooke), Butt, Cole, Keane, Giggs
Rotor Volgograd: Samorukov, Shmarko, Burlatchenko, Berketov, Estchenko (Tsarenko), Junenko, Korniets, Nidergaus (Krivov), Veretennikov, Esipov, Zernov (Ilushim)

ROTOR HELL

FERGIE FLOPS WRECKED BY RUSSIAN BLITZ

A stunning Russian double blast sent shellshocked Manchester United crashing out of Europe last night.

United's UEFA Cup dreams were wrecked by two first-half goals by Russian raiders Rotor Volgograd.

And, although a stirring second-half fightback saved their proud 39-year record of never having lost a European match at Old Trafford, Alex Ferguson's side went out on away goals.

Fergie gambled by throwing in rookie defenders John O'Kane and Phil Neville and, in a bid to boost United's goal power, gave early recall to injury victims Roy Keane and Andy Cole.

Incredibly, it was keeper Peter Schmeichel who scored United's late equaliser. He spent much of the last 15 minutes in the Rotor box and headed home a Ryan Giggs corner.

Daily Star, **27 Sept 1995**

UNITED IN £11M EURO WIPEOUT

Manchester United had £11million wiped off the value of their football empire yesterday.

The crippling loss for Old Traffords's money men followed Alex Ferguson's shock UEFA Cup exit at the hands of Russians Rotor Volgograd.
The Sun, **September 28**

PADDY ROCHE

JOHNNY SIVEBAEK   **NIKOLA JOVANOVIC**   **GRAEME HOGG**   **MAL DONAGHY**

MIKE PHELAN   **COLIN GIBSON**   **RALPH MILNE**

TED MacDOUGALL   **GARRY BIRTLES**   **TERRY GIBSON**

If you had to hand pick a
Manchester United side to play against
your own favourite team, could you do
any better – or worse – than this?

Sub   **PETER DAVENPORT**   Manager   **FRANK O'FARRELL**

Tottenham Hotspur	4	1	Manchester United

Sheringham, Campbell, Armstrong 2   32,852   Cole

1995–6 season – 1 January 1996

The man who had the greatest influence on this match was United's forgotten second Frenchman William Prunier, who had made his debut two days earlier. This match was to be his last. The answer to all United's defensive problems proved to be completely out of his depth.

The bald Frenchman's nightmare was completed when Andy Cole scored with a scissors kick only for Prunier to be penalised for a push. It was the only goal he prevented all afternoon. The following day, he was on his way back to France, never to be heard of again. Yet he will always have a place in our hearts.

Tottenham Hotspur: Walker, Austin, Calderwood, Nethercott, Edinburgh, Rosenthal, Campbell, Caskey, Dumitrescu (McMahon), Armstrong, Sheringham
Manchester United: Schmeichel (Pilkington), Parker, G. Neville, Prunier, P. Neville (Sharpe), Beckham, Butt, Keane (McClair), Giggs, Cantona, Cole

ARMSTRONG CUTS DOWN UNITED

New Year's Day is Manchester United's undoing. They came apart at the seams, their makeshift defence torn asunder by Tottenham Hotspur last night in their biggest defeat since the first day of 1992, when they lost by the same score to Queen's Park Rangers

"The gods are conspiring against us just now," Alex Ferguson, the United manager, said. "Paul Scholes was taken ill during the warm-up, then, when Schmeichel came into the dressing-room just 10 to 15 minutes before the kick-off, he said that he had pulled a calf muscle. You are always going to be under pressure and we didn't have the material to handle it."
Rob Hughes, *The Times*, 2 Jan 1996

TWO-GOAL ARMSTRONG SPELLS TROUBLE FOR GENEROUS UNITED

United can claim they were without their first-choice back four while Peter Schmeichel, who had a calf injury, was replaced at half-time by Kevin Pilkington. It must also be said that on the evidence of last night, William Prunier, the triallist from Bordeaux, did not look a championship-winning centre-half. He preferred to mark space rather than players but Tottenham kept playing the ball to Teddy Sheringham and Chris Armstrong rather than into space.
***Daily Telegraph*, 2 Jan 1996**

MONEY WELL SPENT 2

WYN DAVIES

- - - - - - - - - - - - - - -

BEFORE

Rangy and much-travelled Welsh centre-forward, whose goals and wholehearted endeavour in a Newcastle shirt soon earned him the status of a cult.

NIKOLA JOVANOVIC

- - - - - - - - - - - - - - -

BEFORE

Cetinje-born, sure-footed and versatile centre-half, stopper and pivot, who rapidly earned his reputation with Yugoslav Army outfit Red Star Belgrade.

KAREL POBORSKY

- - - - - - - - - - - - - - -

BEFORE

Lank-haired flankman of scheming proportions, who hails from Jindinchuv-Hadec. His wonder goal for the Czech Republic against Portuguese opponents established him on the world stage.

DANNY WALLACE

- - - - - - - - - - - - - - -

BEFORE

Chunky dynamo, whose ability to go past defenders as if they weren't there soon caught the eye, as did his record of 62 League goals in six seasons.

GEORGE GRAHAM

- - - - - - - - - - - - - - -

BEFORE

A foraging inside-forward, with middle-line operating skills, who plied an honest trade with Chelsea, Aston Villa and Arsenal. Scored half a goal for the Gunners – along with Eddie Kelly – in the 1971 FA Cup Final.

TED MacDOUGALL

- - - - - - - - - - - - - - -

BEFORE

Prolific goal-getter, notching 103 in 146 League starts for Third Division Bournemouth, scoring a record nine goals in one FA Cup tie against Margate in 1971.

IAN STOREY-MOORE

- - - - - - - - - - - - - - -

BEFORE

Opportunist, double-barrelled striker, he earned several names for himself in poaching over 100 goals in a Nottingham Forest shirt and even earning full England honours against Holland in 1970.

NEIL WEBB

- - - - - - - - - - - - - - -

BEFORE

Languid and adept wing-half, who could always be relied on to score goals at the right time. Soon became renowned for his quick-thinking and opportunism.

MONEY WELL SPENT 2

WYN DAVIES

AFTER
Rangy, long-in-the-tooth Welshman in the forward berth, whose lack of goals and cult status at Old Trafford soon earned him a Blackpool shirt.

NIKOLA JOVANOVIC

AFTER
Cetinje-born, leaden-footed and inflexible footballer, following his £300,000 capture from the Balkans. He rapidly earned a reputation after his first call up to the United colours against Ipswich.

KAREL POBORSKY

AFTER
Inconsistent bench-warmer, who rippled the net on a mere three occasions for United, and soon became a favourite among visiting fans. Joined Benfica in search of more Portuguese opponents.

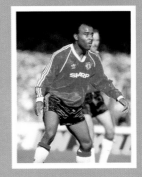

DANNY WALLACE

AFTER
Extremely chunky dynamo, whose new-found inability to go past defenders soon caught the eye, as did his record of six League goals in five seasons.

GEORGE GRAHAM

AFTER
Secured from Highbury when United looked like being relegated. Stayed long enough to finish the job, and skipper the side into the lower ranks.

TED MacDOUGALL

AFTER
After scoring just five times in his United career, he failed to establish himself as a top-flight poacher, although he did finally recapture his Bournemouth form back at Bournemouth.

IAN STOREY-MOORE

AFTER
Added to the ranks for a then massive £200,000 in 1972, in his first full season his goals tally barely exceeded the total number of his names. His career was cut short by injury after 11 goals in two campaigns.

NEIL WEBB

AFTER
Slow and inept schemer, who could always be relied on to get injured at the wrong time. Soon became renowned for his quick-thinking and elegant wife.

CANTONA:

To: Mr Eric Cantona, Screenwriter, Director, Producer, Actor, Scene-painter
From: Elmer J. Schweinbacker III Assistant Scriptreader, Pan-Global Movie Inc.

Dear Mr Cantona,

Thank you for your screenplay for the movie *Cantona: A Genius*. We kinda like this here at Pan-Global. We see this as another *Citizen Kane* or *Police Academy V*. It has pizzazz, class, sophistication and unnecessary violence. It's so refreshing to discover a new talent like yourself bursting on to the scene, coming as you do from a non-movie-making country like France. What have you been doing all these years? Your script is perfect in every way and we wouldn't alter a single word. However, can I suggest one or two changes, before we commit ourselves to your proposed $200 million budget?

Firstly let me say, we love the *kung fu* element. The *kung fu* works. The vigilante plot works. We love a guy who takes the law into his own hands. Everyone in the movie except the hero seems to be an English bad guy – which will go down great over here. We're just not sure about the soccer. I'm afraid soccer doesn't have worldwide appeal in America. We thought maybe you should seriously consider changing from soccer to a major sport like basketball, rollerblading or truck racing.

Also the dialogue. There's just too much of it. Jeez, this guy's long-winded. For instance, that scene where the hero Eric scores the winning field goal in the FA Superbowl and immediately celebrates by writing a poem. And that line about playing football (football? Don't you mean soccer, Eric?). The guy says it's like being married to the most beautiful woman in the world. OK, so why don't we just have the most goddamned beautiful girl in the world, stripped off in the team-tub? This would also clear up the problem we have here with a lot of guys buck naked in the bath together.

Looking forward to working with you,

Elmer

From: Eric Cantona, Genius
To: Elmer J. Schweinbacker, Fool

How could I have believed that a petty-minded simpleton like yourself could ever comprehend my art? It is like asking a candlestick to explain a rainbow to a pigeon. Or something like this.
As Rimbaud said, 'I, purples, coughed up blood, laughter of beautiful lips in anger.' Now perhaps you understand.
By the way, *òu est la cheque magnifique?*

Eric

A GENIUS

FAX
To: Mr Eric Cantona, Screenwriter, Director, Producer, Actor, Scene-painter
From: Elmer J. Schweinbacker III Studio Network Executive, Pan-Global Movie Inc.

Eric,
The guy I got to read your fax kinda sensed a little hostility. Do you want to talk about it, perhaps in words we can understand?
We've now done some extensive market testing on your script by showing it to the pool maintenance man and the Filipino lady who does my laundry. Neither of them can speak proper English, of course, but then again neither can you, feller. They hated the Scotch English team coach guy with the watch-obsession. Why not make him someone we can all relate to – like an American? Also, throughout the script, you appear to have mis-spelt Rambo as Rimbaud.
Another thing. Having got one of my other people to read the script again, we have a problem with your central character. Much as we love the violence, most of it – no, for crying out loud, all of it – seems to be provoked by him. In Hollywood, our heroes really need to be in some way good. This guy's just a schmuck. Stamping on that defenceless tight-end from the Swindon Red Sox – no way buddy.
Incidentally, a different one of my people phoned up Manchester United Soccer Franchise and they said they'd never heard of you.

Elmer

FAX
From: Eric Cantona, Genius
To: Elmer J. Schweinbacker, Idiot, Idiot, Idiot

When the great crested grebe
Dives in the reeds,
Hope becomes a crofter's lament
And the clouds echo the words,
'Where's my money?'

Eric

FAX
To: Mr Eric Cantona
From: Elmer J. Schweinbacker II Executive in Charge of Production, Pan-Global Movie Inc.

There once was a loser from France
Whose script set my eyes in a trance
He may have played soccer
But he's a dumb motherf★★★★★
And we ain't boosting his bank balance

Don't ever contact us again ever, under any circumstances.
Hope we have the pleasure of working with you in the future.

Elmer

The United faithful sway and heave in anticipation. Our bodies tightly packed together, shoulder to shoulder. A young boy is lifted above the throng, so he can get a clearer view. Then suddenly a roar goes up and the crowd surges forward as one. This is the moment we've all been waiting for. 'New away kit on sale now.' Only £49.99 each, children's sizes £59.99,' shouts the woman behind the counter, and I reach inside my United puffa jacket for my Eurocheques. Being in the United Superstore reminds me of the old days — on the Stretford End before they put the seats in.

Just half an hour later, and several thousand krone lighter, I manage to relocate my friends and fellow United loyalists, Tomas, Olaf and Lars-Bobby. They are not difficult to spot, as they are the only ones around carrying three heavy bags of merchandise who are also carrying a Norwegian flag with 'Alex Ferguson's Viking Army' written on it. Some might think we spend too much money, but who can blame us for buying so many things? These bargain prices are impossible to ignore. Also, we have to take advantage, as we live so far away. It's not like we can come to the Theatre Of Dreams every day, like a supporter living in Basingstoke or Welwyn Garden City. We only get to come here once a fortnight for the home games. Although happily, whenever we come to Old Trafford, there is always something new to buy.

Some of our friends back home tease us about coming to England so often, but what can you expect from Arsenal fans?

The train journey to Bergen, the expensive lager drinking, the ferry to Newcastle, the cheap lager drinking, the train journey to Manchester, the reasonably-priced lager drinking, the cost of the souvenirs and the match ticket. No. I have worked it out, and it is still cheaper than spending a night out hanging round Oslo.

With just two hours to go until the kick-off, it is time to make our way to our seats. It's good to see all the familiar faces sitting in their usual places. I wave to Jacques who always makes the short trip from Antwerp.

And there's Andreas giving a thumbs up, looking not too tired after his slightly longer trip from Salonika. And it's great to see Wladislaw, who has made the difficult journey from Chorlton-cum-Hardy. Those Manchester buses can be terrible.

The Stretford End don't start singing until half an hour before the match starts. They bait the opposition fans with cries of 'You're going home in a St Johns Ambulance.' I never cease to be appalled by this chant. Surely they are aware that they should be using the future present tense, 'You will be going home in a St John's Ambulance.' I also dislike it when the fans sing 'There's only one Ronnie Johnsen' – back in Norway, there are three Ronnie Johnsens in my street alone. Although they are correct in their assumption that 'There is only one Ole Gunnar Solskjaer.'

As the match is about to kick off, Lars-Bobby asks me how I think the match will go, but my mind is elsewhere. I have suddenly realised that I forgot to check if the new away bobble hat is in stock ...

MANAGER
RON ATKINSON

1981–6

Aloof O'Farrell, flamboyant Docherty, aloof Sexton: it was flamboyant's turn again. And sure enough, the United board chose Ron Atkinson. Big Ron wasn't exactly the club's first choice, however. In fact, he wasn't even their second or third choice. At the time, the club preferred the hyper-aloof Ron Saunders, the semi-flamboyant Lawrie McMenemy, and the Ipswich Town manager Bobby Robson. Everyone said thanks but no thanks, until Big Ron came along and said thanks and yes please.

United now laboured under the burden of having toiled for fourteen years without winning the League title. During his first four seasons in charge, Big Ron consistently kept Manchester United in the top five, without them ever looking like genuine challengers, let alone threatening Liverpool's overall supremacy. Between 1982 and 1985, the championship took up permanent residence on Merseyside, while United lost out in the battle for the minor placings to the likes of Southampton, Watford and – most humiliatingly – Spurs.

By now United's burden – eighteen years since they last won the League – had turned into a millstone round Atkinson's neck. But not before Big Ron had it expertly polished and set in a solid gold chain.

Everything changed at the start of the 1985–6 season. With ten straight wins, the nearly-men were suddenly transformed into racing certainties for the title, yet, from a seemingly unassailable position, United somehow contrived to throw the title away. From the way they played in the remainder of the season, it appeared that their main ambition was to finish in their customary 4th place, and to this end they were spectacularly successful.

After this astonishing collapse, and with the Championship once again residing at Anfield, Atkinson was living on borrowed time. In fact he admitted later that he should have resigned at the end of the season.

Atkinson's record in the transfer market and ability to judge players was questionable. In his time at Old Trafford, he genuinely believed that the likes of Alan Brazil, John Sivebaek, Peter Davenport and John Gidman were vital cogs in a Championship winning machine. He was also utterly convinced that buying players called Gibson was the key to success – how else can one explain his acquisition of Terry and Colin?

Big Ron's biggest gaffe in his wheeling and dealing was the transfer of Mark Hughes to Barcelona. The deal for the following season was announced in March 1986, when United – in theory at least – were still in a championship race. Hughes never really wanted to go. He and the supporters felt betrayed, and morale sank almost as quickly as the team. The money from the sale was used to buy inferior players.

The bond between Atkinson and the fans was broken for good – a bond that had never been that strong in the first place. Perhaps they never came to terms with the idea of a flash Scouser managing their beloved Manchester United.

While things went badly on the field, off it they got worse. Atkinson's man-management style was hands-off to say the least. Players went on a legendary drinking bout in Amsterdam, and further tales of drunkenness among the squad did the rounds. A training-ground fight between Remi Moses and Jesper Olsen was witnessed by journalists, who were later told by Big Ron that it had never happened. All this created the impression of a gaffe-prone gaffer, who had lost control.

The £4m Flop

That may be Ron's only title this season.

Daily Star,
11 March 1986

If Manchester United couldn't win the title with a ten-point lead, they certainly weren't going to win it from 19th place, which is where they found themselves in early November 1986. Crowds were down by over 10,000. A Littlewoods Cup 3rd round replay at Southampton proved to be the final glittery nail in his spangly coffin. United were dealt a 4–1 spanking and within two days, to the surprise of no one, Atkinson was shown the door. United were so swift to replace him, it was fortunate he didn't meet Alex Ferguson coming in as he was on his way out.

BIG RON'S REVENGE PART 1

Sheffield Wednesday	1	0	Manchester United

Sheridan   80,000

Rumbelows Cup Final, 21 April 1991

Manchester United:
Sealey, Irwin, Blackmore, Bruce, Webb (Phelan), Pallister, Robson, Ince, McClair, Hughes, Sharpe
Sheffield Wednesday:
Turner, Nilsson, King, Harkes (Madden), Shirtliff, Pearson, Wilson, Sheridan, Hurst, Williams, Worthington

WISE OWLS CLIP UNITED'S WING

Manchester United forgot yesterday that Owls can sleep with one eye open. As a result, the League Cup has gone to a Second Division club for the first time in 16 years, Sheffield Wednesday deservedly winning a Rumbelows final at Wembley which struggled to stay awake until John Sheridan scored what proved to be the winning goal seven minutes before half-time.

It was a heart-warming victory for a Wednesday side who seem likely to regain their First Division status at the initial attempt and yesterday gave a performance which suggested that they will be no more out of place in the higher section than they looked before for much of the time before coming down last year. Ron Atkinson's faith in the passing game and the former Manchester United manager's tactic of containment and counter-attack has brought Hillsborough its first success at Wembley for 56 years.
Guardian,
22 April 1991

Aston Villa	3	1	Manchester United

Atkinson, Saunders 2 (1 pen.)　　　77,231　　　Hughes

Coca-Cola Cup Final, 27 March 1994

These days United show such contempt for the League Cup that it's easy to forget how desperate they were to win the one domestic trophy that had eluded them (apart from the Auto Windscreens Shield – the one trophy we wouldn't mind them winning).

In 1991, they must have expected to lay their bogey to rest against Second Division Sheffield Wednesday. However the manager who'd lost United the Milk Cup against Liverpool eight years earlier also made sure they lost the Rumbelows Cup Final in 1991 and the Coca-Cola Cup Final three years later. By leading teams to these two trophies, Ron Atkinson won as much silverware against Manchester United as he did in his five seasons at Old Trafford.

The 1993–4 season was a time of fear and loathing for Man United haters everywhere, as for a few anxious weeks United appeared to be heading for a nightmare treble of domestic honours. The newspapers talked of little else, until Big Ron gave us all one day off from reading about the media's love affair with Manchester United.

Yes, there was a last-minute goal. Yes, a penalty was given. The shock was that both the penalty and the goal went to Aston Villa.

Aston Villa: Bosnich, Barrett, Staunton (Sub, Cox), Teale, McGrath, Richardson, Daley, Townsend, Saunders, Atkinson, Fenton
Man Utd: Sealey, Parker, Irwin, Bruce (McClair), Kanchelskis, Pallister, Cantona, Ince, Keane, Hughes, Giggs (Sharpe)

VILLA END UNITED'S DREAM OF THE TREBLE

Manchester United's dream of the treble is over, after they were outplayed and outfought by Aston Villa, who clinched a place in next season's UEFA Cup with a thoroughly deserved victory.

To add to United's troubles, Andrei Kanchelskis became their fourth player to be sent off in five games.

Villa took the lead in the 25th minute when Andy Townsend slipped the ball through to Dean Saunders whose first time touch freed Atkinson. Paul Parker played the Villa forward onside and he beat Les Sealey, playing for the suspended Peter Schmeichel, for his sixth goal in the competition this season.

Richardson's free kick, awarded for Parker's foul on Daley, was met by Saunders at the near post, and the slightest of touches by the Welshman's left foot sent the ball wide of Sealey.

United pressed forward, but Villa did not buckle. On a swift counter attack Daley's shot hit an upright and from the rebound Atkinson's effort was handled on the line by Kanchelskis. Keith Cooper showed Kanchelskis the red card, Saunders converted the resulting penalty, to give Villa an unlikely 3-1 win.

Daily Telegraph, 28 March 1994

ARSENAL v MAN UNITED

Traditionally, Manchester United fans hate Liverpool, despise Leeds and take pity on Manchester City. For the United players, it seems, it's Arsenal they can't stand – and the feeling is mutual.

McClair versus Winterburn, February 1988

In the dying moments of an FA Cup 5th round tie, United are 2–1 down at Highbury, when they are awarded a predictable last-minute penalty. Up steps Brian McClair, who promptly balloons it over the bar. Up then steps Nigel Winterburn to comfort McClair, by clapping him on both cheeks. McClair, who might have preferred a comforting arm around the shoulder, decides to comfort Winterburn with his fists.

Eleven men versus ten, October 1990

After taking a break from fighting for a couple of seasons, the two teams more than make up for lost time with an epic set-to at Old Trafford. Arsenal keeper David Seaman brings an otherwise splendid scrap into disrepute by failing to become involved. The match finally ends 2–1 to Arsenal – two points deducted to United's one.

Schmeichel versus Wright, November 1996 (part 1) February 1997 (part 2)

After Ian Wright is booked for a late challenge on Peter Schmeichel, he alleges that the Dane retaliated with racist remarks. In the return fixture three months later, the two are face to face once more. Schmeichel is about to collect the ball after an offside decision, when Wright chooses this moment to show the United goalie who sponsors his studs by lunging in with both feet. Schmeichel is later reported to have run up to him at the final whistle and said, 'You're still a dirty black bastard.' Schmeichel has strongly denied that anything racist was said.

Wenger versus Ferguson, April 1997

Alex Ferguson's appeals to have the football season extended – presumably to tie in with the policy on matches – were challenged by Arsenal's manager Arséne Wenger. Alex Ferguson responded in typical fashion on *Match Of The Day*. 'He's come here from Japan and he's telling English people how to organise our football,' said the Scotsman.

Everton	1	0	Manchester United

Rideout   **79,592**

FA Cup Final, 20 May 1995

1994–5 was perhaps the greatest season of the modern era, as United lost the Championship to Blackburn on the last day of the League programme, then six days later lost the Cup Final to Everton. United fans' taunts about how easy it would be to retain the Double turned out to be about as empty as the United trophy cabinet that season.

Everton: Southall, Jackson, Watson, Unsworth, Ablett, Limpar (Amokachi), Parkinson, Horne, Hinchcliffe, Stuart, Rideout (Ferguson)
Manchester United: Schmeichel, G.Neville, Bruce (Giggs), Pallister, Irwin, Butt, Keane, Ince, Sharpe (Scholes), McClair, Hughes

CANTONA COST US THE LOT

Alex Ferguson, the man who has savoured the sweet taste of trophy success six times in nine years as Manchester United boss, was last night suffering from total devastation.

And the Glaswegian pointed the finger at Eric Cantona's departure from his squad – after that infamous Kung Fu kick at a Crystal Palace fan – as the main reason for this season's dismal conclusion.

Last night Ferguson said: "The FA's decision on Eric Cantona was always bad for us – it has probably cost us everything."

All inside six savage days, Fergie saw his Old Trafford All-Stars lose their Championship crown to Blackburn Rovers by a slender point and then the FA Cup to Everton by a single goal.

Sunday Mirror, 21 May 1995

DRUBBINGS – 13

Newcastle United	5	0	Manchester United

Peacock, Ginola, Ferdinand,   36,579
Shearer, Albert

1996–7 season – 20 October 1996

On 11 August, Manchester United beat Newcastle 4–0 in the Charity Shield, and to some media pundits the season was over before it had even begun. Just over two months later, Newcastle had their revenge, and with Philippe Albert's superb lob for the fifth, they effectively won the tie 5–4 on aggregate.

    This was the first time any team managed by Alex Ferguson had lost by five goals.

Newcastle United: Srnicek, Watson (Barton), Albert, Peacock, Beresford, Lee (Clark), Batty, Beardsley, Ginola, Shearer, Ferdinand
Manchester United: Schmeichel, G. Neville, May, Pallister, Irwin, Poborsky (Scholes), Beckham, Johnsen (McClair), Butt, Solskjaer (Cruyff), Cantona

NEWCASTLE OPEN FLOODGATES

Schmeichel had gone nine hours and nine minutes undefeated before his goal fell yesterday in the thirteenth minute. The move began when Beckham gave the ball away to Ginola. He danced past Gary Neville, withstood the barging of Beckham and passed to Ferdinand, whose shot was deflected for a corner.

    Ginola took it, Shearer outjumped the defence and Peacock headed down towards the goal. Irwin scooped the ball away from beneath the bar, but, as television technology was to prove, referee Dunn rightly ruled that it had crossed the goal-line.

    The inevitable arguments led to Schmeichel's booking, but, although a Cantona free kick was to float alarmingly close to Srnicek's own bar, on the half-hour Ginola was to score a sublime second goal, and there was not a semblance of doubt about its quality or its merit.

    Ginola turned on the left-hand edge of the penalty box and, with his right foot, hit the ball across Schmeichel, angled and arrowed for the inside of the far post.

    Keegan loved it – *loved* it! Ferguson of course, did not.

**Rob Hughes, *The Times*,
21 October 1996**

Southampton	6	3	Manchester United

Berkovic 2, Le Tissier, Ostenstad 3   15,256   Beckham, May, Scholes

1996–7 season – 26 October 1996

After the Newcastle match, things just couldn't get any worse … or could they? If Bogart and Bergman always had Paris, the rest of us will always have the week Manchester United shipped 11 goals in two matches.

The year before, United's excuse for the 3–1 defeat at The Dell was that they couldn't see each other in their grey shirts. On this occasion, amazingly, they didn't attribute their humiliation to their blue-and-white shirts.

This was the first time any team managed by Alex Ferguson had conceded six goals.

Southampton: Beasant, Lundekvam, Van Gobbel, Dryden, Oakley, Berkovic, Dodd, Neilson (Magilton), Charlton, (Potter), Le Tissier (Watson), Ostenstad
Manchester United: Schmeichel, G.Neville, May, Pallister (Irwin), P.Neville, Beckham, Butt (McClair), Keane, Cruyff (Solskjaer), Cantona, Scholes

STUNNED UNITED'S NEW LOW

Roy Keane was sent off, Eric Cantona could have joined him and Peter Schmeichel let in six.

And United thought 5-0 at Newcastle was bad.
Sunday Express, 27 October 1996

UNITED THEY FALL AS SAINTS HIT SIX

Southampton fans were baiting United with the chant of "Have you got another kit?"
Independent, 27 October 1996

UNITED PRIDE THAT NEEDED PRICKING

Up and down the country yesterday morning small boys went back to school after the half-term holiday to be greeted with a gleeful taunt: "Five-nil...six-three...five-nil...six-three."

Alex Ferguson, as we know, is not a good loser. He greets defeat with a scowl and, if pushed to discuss it further on terms that do not fit his own views, a snarl. On Saturday he left The Dell without talking to the assembled newspaper reporters, which notionally deprived them of his views but in fact probably saved everyone concerned yet another example of his famous red rages.
Guardian, 29 October 1996

40p tip of Mean United

MANCHESTER United aces knocked back £150 of booze in two hours yesterday . . . then gave pub staff a 40 PENCE tip.

From 2 p.m. to 4 p.m. the 13 soccer tipplers, valued at £75 million and earning an average £10,000 a week, supped Guinness and strong lager to launch their Christmas pub crawl.

But the two 20p pieces the guzzling group left behind led workers at O'Shea's Irish Bar in Manchester to brand them Superstar Scrooges.

Insult

One barman moaned, 'A 40p tip between four staff was an insult. These guys get more in a week than some of us do in a year.'

The players out celebrating – less than 24 hours after their 1-0 win over Aston Villa – included Ryan Giggs, David Beckham and Teddy Sheringham.

Later the tipsy table toppers met up with Andy Cole and Ole Gunnar Solskjaer for a Champagne nosh at Bill Wyman's Sticky Fingers restaurant . . . before going on for more plonk at a private party at a club.

Daily Star,
18 December 1997

Teenage star waited 40 years for United's call

ROY SUTCLIFFE thought he had played pretty well in a trial for Manchester United when, as a teenager, he tried out for the Busby Babes in the summer of 1950.

For weeks he waited for the postman to deliver the summons to Old Trafford that could have meant a glorious career alongside United stars such as Bobby Charlton and Wilf McGuinness.

Mr Sutcliffe, an old fashioned winger in the Manchester Federation Lads League, spent more than 40 years believing he had failed to make the grade. It was only shortly before his mother died three years ago that he discovered he could have been a contender for the No 11 shirt after all.

Mabel Sutcliffe told him she had a letter for him. It was from Jimmy Murphy, Sir Matt Busby's talent scout, asking him to go back so that they could have another look at him.

She had, apparently, forgotten to give it to him. Mr Sutcliffe, now 63, said, 'I opened it up and suddenly realised what had happened to my big chance. It must have come while I was out and my mum just put it in a drawer or something. . .'

The letter carried a Manchester United FC Ltd letterhead and was hand written.

Russell Jenkins, *The Times*, 14 November 1997

Old Trafford fans 'shriek in terror as aliens hover'

The British media seem to have missed one of the biggest stories of the year.

More than 47,000 soccer fans were scared out of their wits and screamed in panic as a UFO hovered above them. Within seconds all 47,000 were pointing towards the sky and shrieking in terror. Players were 'running in a frantic daze', aware that they were being watched by aliens.

Where did all this happen? At Old Trafford, during a recent Manchester United fixture, according to that fount of all knowledge, the *National Enquirer*.

The American newspaper has eye-witness evidence from a Manchester United rooter (sic) and a photographer called Sergio Rubiano, who provides the four pictures which accompany the report under the headline: 'Starship Spectacular! 47,000 ballpark fans see UFO'.

Sounds like something for the *Sunday Sport* to look into.

Daily Telegraph, 23 March 1992

United are sent off by a Red Card

BACKERS of the non-league soccer club Chelmsford City have scored a victory against the premiership giants Manchester United over an advertisement for the soft drink Red Card.

A poster for Red Card, which calls itself a high-energy drink, featured the part-time players of Chelmsford City and the slogan, 'If you can smell fear, Man Utd must reek'. . . United complained to the Advertising Standards Authority that the advertisement 'could provoke antisocial behaviour, unfairly attacked the reputation of Manchester United and made unfair use of the goodwill attached to the club's name.'

Although the authority conceded that the poster might be seen as encouraging rivalry between fans of the two teams, it thought that it was unlikely to cause serious or widespread offence or to encourage antisocial behaviour, and rejected the complaint.

Alexandra Frean, The Times, 22 March 1997

OOH! AH! CONNED YOU ARE

ALUN, 19, TELLS WORLD MAN UTD HAVE SIGNED HIM FOR £500,000

BUT IT'S ALL A FANTASY – HE CAN'T EVEN GET IN SUNDAY LEAGUE SIDE

A village rolled out the red carpet for a local soccer player after he revealed: 'I've been signed up by Manchester United for £500,000.'

Alun McGorian, 19, became the toast of his pals as news of his move spread.

Mum Marilyn, 39, hung a banner outside her home proclaiming, 'Well done Alun – Man Utd number one.' . . .

But yesterday, it was revealed that Alun was not so much a Red Devil as a **CHEEKY** Devil. . . .

But Alun was unrepentant yesterday, saying: 'Yes, I've signed for United and I'm off to Old Trafford now.'

The Sun, 18 May 1996

Côtes du Cantona – a pretentious red, with an unexpected kick, which will be gone before you know it.

'Two men nicknamed The Wizard of the Dribble but for totally different reasons'.

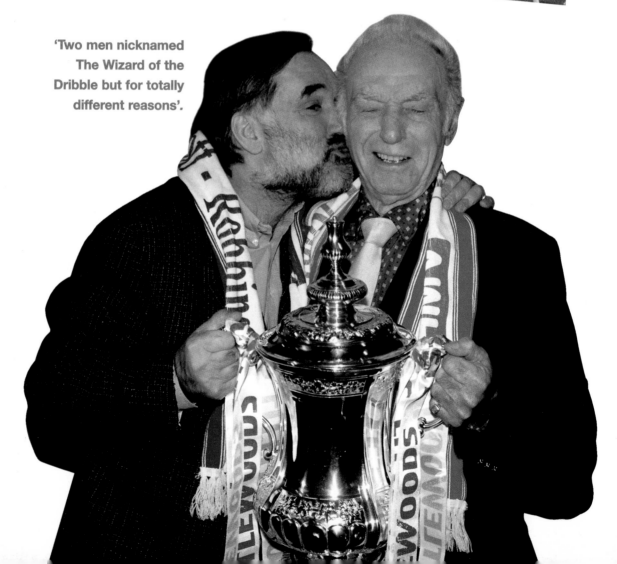

Manchester United	0	3	York City

29,049   Barnes 2 (1 pen.), Barras

Coca-Cola Cup 2nd round 1st leg, 20 September 1995

Man United fans like to dismiss this inept display, on the grounds that they fielded only a second team. However, not many reserve sides include Irwin, Phil Neville, Pallister, Bruce, Sharpe, Beckham and Giggs. The fact is that this was a huge miscalculation on Alex Ferguson's part; he foolishly assumed a team containing eight internationals would be good enough to beat the side then lying in 23rd place in the Second Division.

After the match, Ferguson promised, 'The big guns will be out for the second leg', and they certainly were out – 4-3 on aggregate

Manchester United: Pilkington, Parker, Irwin, McGibbon, Sharpe, Pallister, P. Neville (Cooke) Beckham, McClair, Davies (Bruce), Giggs
York City: Kiely, McMillan, Hall, Pepper, Tutill, Barras, Murty, Williams, Barnes, Peverell (Baker), Jordan

YORK SURPRISE MIGHTY UNITED

OLD TRAFFORD LEFT STUNNED AS YORK TEACH UNITED A LESSON

Manchester United suffered an embarrassing 3-0 home defeat against Second Division strugglers York City in the first leg of their second round Coca-Cola Cup tie last night.

York, who collected their first League win of the season at Swansea on Saturday, won with two goals from Paul Barnes and one from defender Tony Barras.

York could have been two up in the opening minutes as United's defence looked shaky, but had to wait until the 24th minute to take the lead. Barnes's firmly struck shot took a deflection and squirmed through the grasp of United's reserve goalkeeper, Kevin Pilkington. Five minutes into the second half McGibbon was sent off for pulling back Barnes who picked himself up to score from the penalty spot.

There was worse to come for United two minutes later as the defence crumbled again, Pilkington hesitated as he came out to challenge for a free-kick and Barras headed home.

Independent, 21 Sept 1995

Big Ron abandons the sun-lamp for a couple of weeks to go on holiday.

The crowds have gone home, the players are in the bar, but Fergie insists there are still a couple of minutes to go.

Manchester United	1	1	Barnsley

Sheringham   74,700   Hendrie

FA Cup 5th round, 15 February 1998

Barnsley	3	2	Manchester United

Hendrie, S Jones 2   18,655   Sheringham, Cole

FA Cup 5th round replay, 25 February 1998

These two matches had everything you could wish for in a Cup tie. Plenty of goals, non-stop action, a hilarious goalkeeping error, an obvious penalty turned down, a huge bust-up, an offside goal, an unlikely hero, a nailbiting finish and, in the end, sweet revenge. And best of all, Manchester United on the wrong end of a Cup upset.

Barnsley, the team relegated by 'experts' the moment they were promoted, had gone down to United in the Premiership by a fluky 7–0 the previous October. When the FA Cup draw paired the two together, United fans were cock-a-hoop, until the match actually started. Barnsley took the lead after Peter Schmeichel sliced a routine back-pass into his own six yard box and then lost a race with John Hendrie to reach it first. Then five minutes from time, following Sheringham's equaliser, Gary Neville upended Barnsley's Andy Liddell in the box for the most obvious penalty of the year. One can only assume the referee didn't have a clear view of the incident. Even Alex Ferguson was shocked when the referee waved play on. Fortunately, he recovered in time to accuse Andy Gray of talking crap for suggesting that United would have got a penalty in the same situation.

All this led to the replay being one of the most eagerly awaited matches of the season, yet little did anyone realise how it would exceed all expectations. Barnsley went one up with a goal that was clearly offside, before adding two more from Scott Jones, a player who that week had been on the verge of joining 3rd Division Mansfield. United got back to 2–3 and had plenty of chances to equalise, especially during the six baffling minutes of injury time.

15.2.98
Manchester United: Schmeichel, Clegg, Irwin, Johnsen (Beckham), Pallister, Sheringham, Giggs, P. Neville, McClair, (G. Neville), Berg, Nevland (Cruyff).
Barnsley: Watson, Eaden, Moses, De Zeeuw (Appleby), Hendrie (Liddell), Redfearn, Bullock, Bosancic, Krizan, Ward, Morgan.

25.2.98
Barnsley: Watson, Appleby, (Sheridan), Moses, Hendrie (Liddell), Redfearn, Bullock (Marcelle), Bosancic, Jones, Barnard, Ward, Markstedt.
Manchester United: Schmeichel, G. Neville, May, Pallister, Beckham, Cole, P. Neville, McClair (Irwin) Nevland (Sheringham), Thornley, Clegg (Twiss).

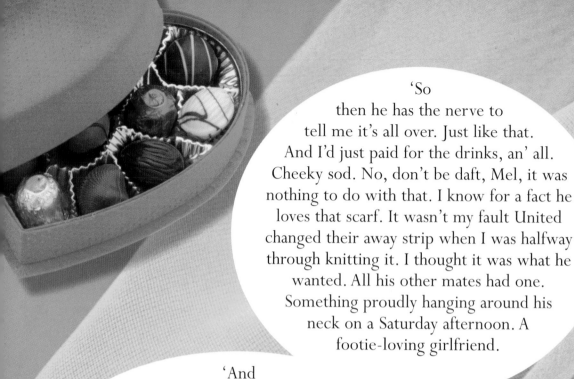

'So then he has the nerve to tell me it's all over. Just like that. And I'd just paid for the drinks, an' all. Cheeky sod. No, don't be daft, Mel, it was nothing to do with that. I know for a fact he loves that scarf. It wasn't my fault United changed their away strip when I was halfway through knitting it. I thought it was what he wanted. All his other mates had one. Something proudly hanging around his neck on a Saturday afternoon. A footie-loving girlfriend.

'And only the other night we enjoyed the most intimate moment two people can possibly share together – when he showed me his programme collection. I said to him, "why don't you stick it in date order" – and that's when he went all funny on me. I'd like to tell him where to stick it now.

'No, Mel, I don't see a pattern. What are you talking about? Trevor was completely different, wasn't he? He liked fishing. God, the hours I spent putting wriggling maggots on hooks for him. I hated him for months before he finally chucked me. Yes of course I remember Kevin. You don't forget dating a pot-holer. God, the hours I spent wriggling along on my stomach through damp caves in the Peak District.

'The
stupid thing, right, is that I was just
beginning to like the bloody game. I could talk back to
him about it, instead of him just talking all the time. All right, I
admit when I first went out with him, I used to giggle every time he'd
sing the praises of David Beckham's long balls. But in the end, I got sick
of all the other girls endlessly arguing over whether Philip Neville or
Gary Neville had the nicer arse. Who cares, as long as they're both
comfortable on the ball coming out of defence? You should
have seen the looks on their faces when I said that.
And the look on his face, mind.

'No,
Mel, I'm certain we'll never get back
together. 'Cos there's one thing I haven't told you. I
came across him the other night in O'Toole's – you know, the
old Rose and Crown – with that slapper Sandra Carey. And do you
know what I heard him say? "It's only the goalkeeper who's allowed
to pick up the ball." How could he, the bastard? That's exactly
what he said to me when he started
chatting me up.

'I
know you'll think I'm soft, but I
am gonna miss him. Do you know, we only
had our first argument the week before last. He
reckoned Solskjaer should always play from the start,
whereas I feel he's most effective coming off the bench.
'Cos I think you'll agree with me, Mel, that football
these days is very much a 14-man game.
Mel? … Mel? … Hello?…
Are you there?'

UNITED IN

Manchester United	0	1	Fenerbahçe

53,297   Bolic

Champions' League group C, 30 October 1996

Manchester United	0	1	Juventus

53,529   Del Piero (pen.)

Champions' League group C, 20 November 1996

Man Utd: Schmeichel, G Neville (P. Neville, Irwin, May, Johnsen, Cantona, Butt, Beckham, Cruyff (Scholes), Poborsky (Solskjaer), Keane
Fenerbahçe: Rustu, Ilker, Uche, Hogh (Bulent), Kemalettin, Tuncay (Mustafa), Bolic (Tarik), Okacha, Kostadinov, Saffet, Erol

Man Utd: Schmeichel, G. Neville, Johnsen, May, P. Neville (McClair), Beckham, Butt, Keane, Giggs, Cantona, Solskjaer (Cruyff)
Juventus: Peruzzi, Torricelli (Juliano), Ferrara, Montero, Porrini, Di Livio (Tacchinardi), Deschamps, Zidane, Jugovic, Boksic, Del Piero

IT'S FERGIE'S EURO FOLLY

In the end, they got what they deserved.

Wicked deflections and near misses notwithstanding, that Alex Ferguson should find himself beaten by a striker called Bolic was cruelly appropriate.

Because, when Fergie dropped his strikers, he dropped something far more serious at Old Trafford. Like the initiative and advantage of playing a team at home, having already defeated them 2-0 away.

Fenerbahçe, humbled on their own doorstep, will not have fancied coming to Old Trafford. By the end, they were playing as if they owned the place.
***The Sun*, 31 October 1996**

TAMED

United went down fighting but they could never overcome the 35th minute penalty that Nicky Butt surrendered to Alessandro Del Piero.

Predictably, Zinedine Zidane was the creator in a French axis with countryman Didier Deschamps, the man Eric Cantona once condemned as merely a "water carrier".

He certainly looked to have the right pedigree to me as the ammunition line delivered the ball to the feet of Del Piero. In an instant, he lay in a crumpled heap at the very corner of Peter Schmeichel's box.
***The Sun*, 21 November 1996**

HUMILIATION

EUROPE – 8, 9 &10

Manchester United	0	1	Borussia Dortmund

53,606   Ricken

Champions' Cup semi-final 2nd leg, 23 April 1997

The year before only a Schmeichel header had preserved Manchester United's proud 40-year unbeaten home record in Europe. United fans were relieved that at least they hadn't lost it to an unheralded side like Rotor Volgograd. If ever they were to lose that unbeaten record, say in another 40 years, it would surely be to the likes of Real Madrid or AC Milan.

One year and one home match later, Manchester United lost that proud unbeaten record to Turkey's Fenerbahçe.

Against Juventus on 20 November, United's proud unbeaten home record in Europe, dating back three weeks, came to an end. Having already been comprehensively outplayed in Turin, they fell to their third defeat in their Champions' League group. Once again, Ferguson's United displayed their customary naivety when stepping up a class, by giving away a first-half penalty.

United had the dubious distinction of becoming the first club to get through to the Champions' Cup semi-final after losing three of their six goup matches. United weren't finished yet – they still had more defeats in them. After going down by a single goal at Borussia Dortmund, they had everything to do in the 2nd leg. And, yes, they lost again.

I don't know. You wait 40 years for one home defeat, and then three come along at once.

Man Utd: Schmeichel, G. Neville, May (Scholes), P. Neville, Johnsen, Pallister, Cantona, Butt, Cole, Beckham, Solskjaer (Giggs)

B. Dortmund: Klos, Reuter (Tretschok), Kohler, Feiersinger, Kree, Ricken (Zorc), Lambert, Moller, Heinrich, Chapuisat, Riedle (Herrlich)

PANICKING UNITED FAIL

The dream is dead and Manchester United are left with the harsh reality that European glory is still some way beyond their desperately grasping fingers.

Beaten home and away by a Dortmund side who epitomise all the qualities needed to establish supremacy in this most prestigious of competitions, Alex Ferguson will know his side were simply not good enough.

From the moment Lars Ricken gave Dortmund the precious cushion of an away goal, United were engulfed in a panicking frenzy of frantic activity which, although promising much, delivered nothing.

Daily Express, **24 April 1997**

WE'RE JUST NOT GOOD ENOUGH

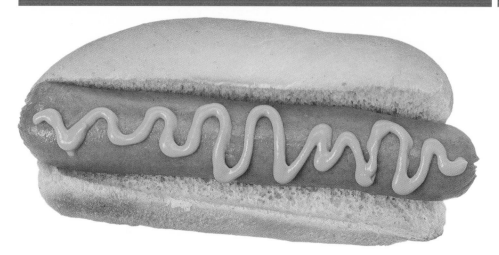

Q. What was Manchester United's dismal excuse for their even more dismal form during the first half of the 1989–90 season?

A. According to the manager, players, fans and the bloke who sells dodgy hot dogs near the ground, the team were distracted by the abortive takeover by Michael Knighton. Otherwise, the players – Ralph Milne, Mike Phelan, Danny Wallace et al – would have romped home in the Championship by Christmas, instead of ending up 11th. Of course, the previous season when they were 10th, the team were naturally too preoccupied with concern for the health and well-being of the infant Princess Beatrice, first-born of the Duchess of York. In 1987–88 (5th), they were overcome by the failure of T'Pau to convincingly follow-up their smash No. 1 hit 'China in your hand'. And so on.

**Q.
Why did Manchester United fail to sign Alan Shearer from Southampton in summer 1992?**

A.
Manchester United plc refused to release enough funds until after 31 July, to tie in with their accounting policies. By that time he'd already joined Blackburn Rovers. United also claimed that Shearer was heavily overpriced at £3.6 million. This didn't stop them bidding £15 million to try and scupper Shearer's move from Blackburn to Newcastle. Alan Shearer's decision to return to his home town club has led him to become a figure of hate among United fans, for daring to spurn the mighty Reds.

# MONEY WELL SPENT 3

Words fail us when it comes to describing these Manchester United players. Perhaps you can help, by choosing from the list of words beneath. Some, but not all, of these descriptions may be appropriate. You decide, by filling in the captions yourself.

MAL DONAGHY

COLIN GIBSON

TERRY GIBSON

RALPH MILNE

MIKE PHELAN

WILLIAM PRUNIER

JOHN SIVEBAEK

CHRIS TURNER

Willing	Gallic	Crab-like	Able
Unwilling	Leaden-footed	Faltering	Unable
Diminutive	Custodian	Nightmarish	Unbelievable
Danish	Stopper	Wholehearted	Crap
Unhurried	Craggy	Adroit	Bloody rubbish
Tireless	Sluggish	Maladroit	For Christ's sake!
Tiresome	Leisurely	Alleged defender	Quite good

SEASON 1997-8

This was the year that Manchester United would bring home the European Cup to its rightful place, on the 30th anniversary of Matt Busby's famous triumph. Never mind those Continental upstarts from Juventus, Ajax and Real Madrid – what did they know about how to win European trophies? Fergie's fledglings had grown up together and were now ready to spread their wings, under the watchful eye of mother hen, and bring back to the Old Trafford nest the twigs and worms that were the Champions' League – whilst comfortably retaining the Premiership, of course.

To start with, it all went according to the official script. Man United stormed through their first five Champions' League fixtures – beating Juventus on the way – and had the media purring their approval. It seemed that the likes of Blackburn, Liverpool and Chelsea were all scrambling for 2nd place. True, they suffered their customary embarrassing League Cup reverse – this time by 2–0 at First Division Ipswich Town – but this left United with one less distraction. With a comfortable cushion in the Premiership (on sale at all United stores), having lost just twice before Christmas, the team was now free to concentrate on the Champions' League. Fortunately, they didn't concentrate very well at all.

Perhaps the first sign that Manchester United hadn't yet reached full maturity was their final Champions' League fixture in Turin, when they appeared happy to play out a goalless draw. A late Juventus goal allowed them to squeak through into the knockout section.

WOBBLE NO. 1

Playing at Coventry in late December, United were cruising to victory when two late goals – including a last-minute solo effort from Darren Huckerby – sent them packing. Then, for the third season running, they lost at Southampton. In the next match, Tony Cottee – who just a couple of weeks earlier had been knocking them in in the Malaysian League – gave Leicester City a 1–0 win at fortress Old Trafford. A week later, they were only five minutes away from losing at home again, to relegation-bound Bolton.

The bizarre outcome of this string of results was that Man United appeared to increase their lead at the top. Not that it seemed to matter. Every time one of United's closest rivals had a chance to narrow the gap, they would predictably lose. United got back on course for the Premiership with three successive wins, leaving them clear at the top and with that cushion as comfortable as ever. Bookmakers suspended bets on the title, and one, the appropriately named Fred Done, paid out £50,000 to punters who had bet on Manchester United.

WOBBLE NO. 2

In two magnificent weeks in March, United's season fell apart. It began with what seemed like a good result – 0–0 away at Monaco. While their thoughts were on preparations for the second leg, they managed to lose tamely at Sheffield Wednesday and only draw at West Ham. Then came a Saturday morning match at home to Arsenal. Due to the quirks of the fixture list, Arsenal had played so many games fewer that people had hardly noticed, until now, that they were in the Championship race or that they had been unbeaten since December. The only goal of the game, by Marc Overmars, meant that suddenly United's cushion had disappeared down the back of the sofa. Four days later, a 1–1 draw at home put Man United out of Europe on away goals, and the fabulous fortnight was complete.

The destiny of the title, for the first time, was in Arsenal's hands not United's. Alex Ferguson – previously the master of psychology – was quick to point out that all the pressure was on the Gunners. Arsenal manager Arséne Wenger had a brilliant new ploy for coping with Ferguson's sniping: he ignored it. In April, while United were stumbling to home draws with Liverpool and Newcastle, Arsenal were demolishing Blackburn 4–1 away and Wimbledon 5–0 at home. On 18 April, Man United lost the leadership of the Premiership for the first time since the previous October. They never regained it.

Perhaps Ferguson should have bought new players. Despite limitless resources, he refused to add new players to his squad, with the exception of the ageing Teddy Sheringham, who by the end of the season was challenging Brian McClair for bench space. Perhaps Europe became too much of an obsession. Perhaps Fergie was losing his touch. But at the end of the day, when all's said and done, in the final analysis ... hurray!

In December, Man United had enjoyed a 13-point lead over Arsenal but still contrived to throw away the title. Those days of squandering massive Championship leads had made a welcome return.

FERGIE GETS THE BOOT

Manchester United bowed to the inevitable today, when Alex Ferguson was sacked as manager after over 14 years at the helm. Andy Cole has been installed as caretaker boss until a candidate can be found who is prepared to take over what has been described as the worst job in football.

Cash-strapped United, currently playing in front of home crowds of less than 5,000, are propping up the 'I CAN'T BELIEVE IT'S NOT BUTTER' First Division. They have failed to register a single victory all season following relegation from the Premiership.

Ferguson's reaction was typical. 'If only I'd been allowed some extra time, I feel sure I could have turned this once great club around. Unfortunately, the decision to build a 200,000-seater stadium in Norfolk, just at the time our support was on the wane, did not help. At least I can hold my head up high in the knowledge that none of it was my fault.'

Captain Brian McClair, ever-present all term, said, 'I feel sorry for him. Maybe it was the pressures of the job that turned him into a complete Bcmdsmvkijvzxjn keazn$£&pratheadvzh?!nxjmcsAJvhnzsnshkjlalmd and that's not an easy thing for me to say.'

Chairman Edwards has promised there will be money to spend for whoever is next in the Old Trafford hot-seat. 'Before we can buy, we need to sell and if that means we lose our best and most consistent players, then so be it. I'll be sorry to see Jordi Cruyff and Stan Collymore leave but that's football.' When pressed about possible successors, the United supremo said, 'I can't say at the moment but suffice to say we are talking to some of the top names in the game.'

| RIOCH | SOUNESS | BALL | WITHE |